GREEN COLLAR JOBS

GREEN COLLAR JOBS

Environmental Careers
for the 21st Century

Scott M. Deitche

Foreword by Tim Center

 PRAEGER

AN IMPRINT OF ABC-CLIO, LLC
Santa Barbara, California • Denver, Colorado • Oxford, England

Library of Congress Cataloging-in-Publication Data

Deitche, Scott M.
  Green collar jobs : environmental careers for the 21st century / Scott M. Deitche.
    p. cm.
  Includes bibliographical references and index.
  ISBN 978-0-313-38014-3 (alk. paper) — ISBN 978-0-313-38015-0 (ebook)
1. Environmental sciences—Vocational guidance. 2. Environmentalism. 3. Industries—Environmental aspects. I. Title.
  GE60.D45 2010
  333.72023—dc22   2009052025

14 13 12 11 10   2 3 4 5

This book is also available on the World Wide Web as an eBook.

Visit www.abc-clio.com for details.

Praeger
An Imprint of ABC-CLIO, LLC

ABC-CLIO, LLC
130 Cremona Drive, P.O. Box 1911
Santa Barbara, California 93116-1911

This book is printed on acid-free paper ∞

Manufactured in the United States of America

CONTENTS

vi   Contents

FOREWORD

One of my favorite drinks growing up was Welch's grape soda. It was always a treat to drink a soda as a kid. And I'd be sure to get every drop from that can, tilting it back and slurping the few remaining drops from its lip. A small feeling of sadness might develop when it was all gone— especially if I was still thirsty. I can tell you that my young daughter has the same impulses.

Well, that soda can is very much like our planet in that it has a finite amount in it—whether it be uranium, oil, natural gas, coal, fish in the ocean, water, or any of the many other natural elements that are used to feed us, to power our homes and businesses, or to make our cell phones, batteries, computers, and so forth.

In fact, according to some studies, at the current rate of our consumption of natural resources, we will need several planets to sustain us. How can we continue to enjoy a quality of life with abundance and opportunity today, while ensuring the same for our kids and their kids?

This brings us to the word *sustainability*, which can mean so much to so many. The Brundtland Commission defined the term in its 1987 report to the United Nations[1] as meeting "the needs of the present without compromising the ability of future generations to meet their own needs." I think the Boy Scouts of America say it a little better—leave your campsite better than you found it. It is perhaps best captured in these three words: *people, planet, profit.*

In this era of going green, reducing our carbon footprint, ending our dependence on foreign oil, and addressing the challenges of climate change, we tend to avoid the real issue. It's really about survivability. And it's not about the survivability of the planet—it's about the survivability of the people who live here. That is why the issue of the green collar economy is so inspiring. It addresses so many of our motivations.

From a business perspective, this issue presents an opportunity to move society into the next revolution—away from the pollution, waste, and toxicity of the industrial revolution—toward clean, renewable, cradle-to-cradle processes that inspire and lighten our demand on natural resources.

I begin with business, because it is often really about money—even when everyone says it isn't. Think about it. Do you have a compact fluorescent lightbulb lighting your home? Yes? Perhaps you have a lot of them. Let me ask you. Did you buy them to save the polar bears? Or did you buy them because (1) someone told you that you would save money on your power bill and (2) they didn't cost too much more than traditional incandescent lightbulbs? The fact that they help us collectively reduce greenhouse gas emissions through reduced demand for energy is a bonus.

Well, look at Unilever—this multinational conglomerate is the largest seller of frozen fish sticks—which has been purchasing from sustainable fisheries for a decade.[2] This is not so they can put a label on the package, but because without fish in the ocean, they have no fish sticks to sell. Marriott Hotels purchased for preservation 1.4 million acres of Brazilian rain forest.[3] With hundreds of properties along the coastlines worldwide, keeping the lungs of the planet healthy might keep sea levels from rising and flooding their resort lobbies.

Environmentally, companies are expected to do more and to respect the communities in which they operate. Thanks to federal regulations of the 1960s and 1970s, companies have implemented environmental management systems, and the economics of environmental impacts are beginning to be included on the balance sheet.

This is perhaps become most obvious in the green building movement. Green building principles help reduce the waste of building resources, the impact on the building site, and the consumption of resources during the operating life of a building—all of these things helps the environment, while helping save money up front and for the long term of the occupant. This results in a win-win-win for the developer, the owner, and the community. Of course the logical way to go is for green building to become known simply as building, as we all adopt a new paradigm.

This brings us back to the people and our community. Sustainable organizations do more than simply take—whether it is the area's natural resources or the talent of its people—from the communities in which they operate. They become an integral component, adding value through contributions to their community. Whether through charitable gifts or community investment, those in the community benefit through opportunity and social capital.

In each of these situations, those engaged in the greening of their organizations are becoming more efficient—reducing expenses, reducing waste, and increasing profits. Employees expand their skill sets. Companies hire employees with specialized training in new areas, and they contract with groups that can help provide additional levels of service.

Once they begin to live green, the organizations begin to offer new lines of business. One example is when a waste stream can become a revenue stream. Another is when accounting firms have identified as a new line of service the audit of companies pledging to reduce greenhouse gas emissions—a fresh take on their audit practice with a green hue.

Hopefully, this provides a greater context—albeit a brief look—for why the green collar economy is so important. We must have a workforce—and a management structure—trained to understand how they can make a meaningful contribution toward economic prosperity and environmental stewardship, both for the organization they work for and for the community in which they live. Sustainable organizations should be more resilient in economic downturns, be able to recruit and retain employees and stakeholders of the highest moral and professional character, and enhance brand awareness by making public their commitments to more than just the bottom line.

As businesses begin to adopt—and report on—the triple bottom line, and the marketplace comes to expect—if not demand—this approach, we return to a common theme. One principle that binds each generation to the next is our sincere desire and hope for a better tomorrow. For the next fiscal year. For the ecosystems that support the flora and fauna and us. And, perhaps, most important, for our grandchildren and beyond.

I encourage you to evaluate how you personally and professionally can adopt and implement the principles offered in the following pages. Collectively, we can have a tremendously positive impact on our economy,

on the environment, and on those with whom we share this incredible
planet.

Tim Center, Esq.
Director, Sustainable Florida—Collins Center
Vice President, Sustainability Initiatives
Collins Center for Public Policy

ACKNOWLEDGMENTS

Thanks to my agent, Gina Pannitieri, for working hard to get the project rolling; the staff at Praeger Books; Tim Center for writing the foreword and sending me interesting and useful green information; my colleagues at GPI Southeast, for support and suggestions; William Tuyn, Elie Araj, Ian Thompson, Will Duggan, John Merlino, Fritz Kreiss, and Pat Millington; the Linkedin.com Clean Techies, Green Marketing, and Green Professionals discussion groups; and to my family for continued support through another book project.

INTRODUCTION

Green jobs. What are they? Why are they on everyone's mind now? Why is every day bringing hundreds of news stories about new green job-training programs and about how green jobs will transform our future? What are the job prospects? What do these green jobs pay? Haven't we heard all of this before? Are green jobs any different from what environmental scientists and engineers have been doing for years?

There are so many questions for a topic that has been so talked about, yet is relatively new. Green jobs are a combination of the traditional environmental science and engineering fields, coupled with an eye toward new regulations and a future of sustainability. Sure, there are predictions of millions of jobs, and there are catch phrases designed to soothe, every time they are spoken. But the reality is that green jobs are becoming the future as we speak. Cutting-edge technology, coupled with entrepreneurial and capitalist zeal, and a healthy dose of science are bringing old factories back to life, spurring innovative new ideas from small companies with a new business model of sustainability and profit, and turning barren plains into fields of windmills. The influence of these green jobs is being felt from the halls of Washington, DC, to small towns in the Rust Belt. And though the rose-colored visions of millions of new jobs may be a lot more wishful thinking than probable reality, the fact is that there are new jobs that didn't exist a decade, or even five years ago. And this change may have profound effects on the workers of the United States and the world.

In the mid 1990s, I started working in the environmental field with a degree in marine biology and a desire to get into fish research. When I started my biologist career in 1995, I had not heard of stormwater regulations, or National Pollution Discharge Elimination System (NPDES) permits, or a host of other water-quality-related issues that were just coming into the spotlight at regulatory agencies. I had a vague idea of some of the new pushes for sustainability, but they hadn't yet permeated the mainstream conscious and were even hard to find in the scientific field. I knew some engineers and biologists who worked for environmental consulting companies. There were also some nongovernmental organizations (NGOs), such as Tampa BayWatch (where my wife worked for seven years) that did restoration work and advanced the idea of environmental stewardship. Talk of wind power, solar energy, and truly green jobs was virtually nonexistent.

By 2001, when I switched positions and turned from fish biology to water quality and stormwater, I started seeing a rising wave. The push for green energy and technologies was still just a whimper, still licking its wounds after the oil crisis push in the late 1970s. The challenges over global warming were just beginning, and the low price of gas was feeding the surge in sport utility vehicle (SUV) sales. But there were new companies starting up to address energy, water, and pollution issues. There were visionary commercial ideas from the hard sciences that needed new marketing avenues to get their product out to the masses. And although those jobs were hard to find back then, by late 2007 and my third career move, to a private environmental consulting company, I was riding the wave into the new paradigm of environmental jobs. It was apparent to me that things were changing and that there were opportunities that just weren't available a few years before. The Web was awash with hundreds of sites with thousands of jobs in new fields, with new demands for skills, and new opportunities for economic advancement. Every week, new laws and local policy changes opened up new avenues for job creation. And references that brought together these disparate groups of information were few and far between. Now, in 2009, you can easily find green marketers pushing products made by green companies, responding to environmental issues, and employing both former auto workers and environmental engineers. What a difference a little less than a decade makes.

Separating the real possibilities from pipe dreams is not always easy. Green jobs won't be everywhere, and they won't replace all regular jobs. In energy, coal and oil will still have a seat at the table for years to come, and the idle car plants of General Motors (GM) are not all going to be churning out solar panels and windmill turbines. Yet there is a huge amount of information out there, from mainstream media reports to scientific journals, all talking about the rise of the green career.

Designed to get through all the clutter and filler material about green jobs, this book is designed to help the new job seeker, career changer, or student who is wondering what to do to get familiar with the trends, find places to get jobs, and identify educational institutions to gain the knowledge needed to compete. Although this book is intended as a resource for people interested in green jobs primarily in the United States and Canada, there are a myriad of similar opportunities across the globe. Developing markets in India, China, Southeast Asia, and South America are embracing green as a viable market career track. Chapter 9 deals with the rest of the world's green career potential. Although each chapter starts with a general discussion of the topic at hand, this book is designed to be as practical as possible for the reader. Instead of an abstract discussion about the philosophical concepts of green, the book gives the reader the lowdown on the current job market, where to go for education, what companies are the leaders in various green career paths, which visionaries lead the pack, where to network, and finally, where to look for a job. With the emergence of any new field, there is always change, and things may shift after the book's release. So even though the guide is designed to be as current and predictive as possible, it also gives the readers sources and avenues to keep up to date on the absolute latest trends in green careers.

At the time of this writing, there are uncertainties regarding the role of the green idea in the context of the current recession. But green is more than the hip, edgy concept it was back in the 1990s. The new green revolution is more entrenched than before, and there is a palpable sense of a paradigm shift among those in the industry. In early 2009, as part of the $787 billion economic stimulus package (The American Recovery and Reinvestment Act), President Obama steered over $40 billion toward environmental projects and green job training. Most of the money is in the form of tax incentives and rebates. Over $1 billion was directed strictly toward green job training. It is expected to be the latest shot in the arm to the growing sector. As more government incentives come online, the private sector and entrepreneurs are moving in to carry the torch.

Green is no longer about just doing the right thing for the environment. Green is taking your business to a new level, by reducing costs and expanding your market. Green is market driven, as new companies are popping up overnight to offer everything from sustainable consulting to developing new machines to address water pollution. Green is entrepreneurial, as new niches are being explored and exploited. And green is still the right thing to do for the environment, missteps notwithstanding (e.g., ethanol). Green jobs are definitely going to be a part of the employment landscape for a long time, and now is the best time to get on board. Find a topic you are interested in, see what training and education are out there, find out where the jobs are, and look for one that's right for you.

CHAPTER 1

THE NEW SPACE RACE

On June 10, 2009, the Pew Charitable Trust released a groundbreaking report on green jobs. It was one of the first real looks at how the green collar economy was affecting the job market. The fact that it took place in the depth of a recession made the findings stand out even more. The study found that from 1998 to 2007 clean energy jobs grew at a faster rate than overall jobs in the United States. By 2007, "more than 68,200 green businesses in all fifty states and the District of Columbia generated 770,000 jobs."[1] The study found that even as the country was in the midst of the worst recession since the Great Depression, clean energy jobs, despite a lack of government funding, were attracting new venture capital and providing both high skill and blue collar jobs across the United States. And even as unemployment was rising, clean energy/green jobs (they included careers from engineers to scientists to machinists to marketers) were shown to be declining more slowly, poised for a rebound when the economy regains strength and companies once again begin to expand.

The Pew report was one of the latest to show that green jobs were becoming more than just a buzzword and hype machine driven by the media. Even though the career paths might not all pan out—a recent study from Spain showed some of the predictions about green job creation to be overblown—there is a palpable sense that a new green collar economy has the potential to be a mirror of the traditional white collar/blue collar economy—not only in the United States, but around the world. And although the goal of any good job is money and stability, job satisfaction is higher in green careers because the very nature of the job gives back to the environment and helps foster a sense of sustainability and stewardship. That sense ultimately drives consumers to look at options from the marketplace that include sustainability—whether it be cars that run on hydrogen fuel cells and electricity with recyclable material car mats and clean emissions, to a coffee mug made of recycled material to hold your fair trade organic coffee made with an energy star coffeemaker and recycled paper filters.

When the Industrial Revolution got underway, it's safe to assume that those original captains of industry could not predict how far or how fast the country, in fact the world, would progress. As the 20th century rolled on, the rate of progress at a technological and industrial level was staggering. But starting in the late 1950s, some scientists began seeing the cost to some of the industrial applications. The first strands of environmental stewardship began to form, and a few sparse rules came into effect to try to stem the seemingly one-way street to ecological errors. By the early 1970s, at the dawn of the environmental movement, there were greater efforts by lawmakers to start to turn the tide of the environmental degradation that was affecting the air and water. Certainly there are environmental concerns about conditions that have improved, such as acid rain, but others, such as climate change, are still potential threats. And in these threats are the seeds for the new green economy and jobs that will transform the 21st century economically and environmentally.

Of all the issues behind a need for a new green economy, global climate change is probably one of the biggest environmental issues currently driving most of the policies for spurring innovation and investment in clean energy and environmental technologies. From this investment, it's hoped that a new sector of the great nationwide economy can be created, one that is modeled on ideas of sustainability and social responsibility. Sure, there are some concerns about the legitimacy of climate change and whether it's completely an anthropogenic-driven phenomenon or simply part of a natural cycle. But the need for a more sustainable way of life will still be there, driven by other far-reaching concerns. Take water resources for example. Pollution adversely impacts the ecology, public health, and economies of water bodies and their communities. Through regulations, as you'll see in a later chapter, communities are working to restore the quality of the waters and reduce surface runoff; in turn, regulation has brought on innovation from companies making products that improve water quality.

Thomas Friedman's 2008 bestseller, *Hot, Flat, and Crowded* went into detail about some of the environmental issues confronting the world. He stated flat out that "continuing with the Dirty Fuels System, in a world that is hot, flat, and crowded, will drive all five trends shaping the Energy-Climate Era—energy supply and demand, climate change, petro dictatorship, biodiversity loss, and energy poverty—to unmanageable extremes."[2] His book was the culmination of the rising tide of concern regarding global climate change and other environmental issues that were coming to roost for the world.

I prefer the term *global climate change* rather than *global warming* for a couple of reasons: chief among them is that the term *global warming* gives the impression that the Earth will warm uniformly and that will be that. In fact, the warming cycle is predicted to disrupt most of the climate patterns across the globe, resulting in some colder winters one year and far warmer the next. The very unpredictability of the climate change effects is one area that opponents and critics of human-made climate change theories jump on when asserting their position. To be sure, there are only models to predict how things will change, but there's no question that the climate is shifting and that the implications can be catastrophic or, at the very least, not that convenient. The problem is that by the time the symptoms start, the chance to change course is long gone. John Holdren, President Obama's science advisor, was quoted in the *New Yorker* as saying, "any reasonable comprehensive and up-to-date look at the evidence makes clear that civilization has already generated dangerous anthropogenic interference in the climate system."[3]

Even if the denialists are correct—that the main driver of the climate change is a natural cycle—there is increasing evidence that human-made actions are speeding up the process past its historic levels. This call to arms has been met with everything from overly zealous demands to wean us off every form of energy, and devolve into a more primitive society, to overly critical calls labeling global climate change a conspiracy and a hoax perpetrated by scientists, to what end is not known. If it's to make money off U.S. citizens, I have neither paid anything to my fellow scientists nor received a check in the mail.

But if climate change is human-made, the actions needed to change direction are within the capability of our technology. And that's in part where the green collar economy really comes in, because, ultimately, a return to a simpler time is neither practical nor desirable for a number of reasons, chief among which is that the quality of life and the life expectancy that people enjoy won't be matched by going back to living fully off the land. The compromise must be a way to continue to evolve as a functioning society while acting with even more of an eye toward sustainability and efficiency in the energy we produce, how we produce it, how we use it, and how much of it we use. Only by embracing the saving power of technology can the green collar economy really take off and be that part of the our society that we need it to be.

But there is a more practical reason for embracing sustainability. Climate change has immediate implications for seaside and coastal communities, places where a majority of the world's population lives. Many island countries in the south Pacific are already seeing the effects of rising and fluctuating sea level changes as their countries are slowly being swallowed up by the sea. In the Arctic areas of Canada, many indigenous people are seeing warmer winters, with less ice and higher seas. This is affecting their traditional ways of life, and they are going to have to adapt to the changes or fall victim to the climate. Rising sea levels can also have implications for drinking water supplies. As the sea level rises, the salt water has the potential to infiltrate the aquifer and turn the freshwater supply of groundwater into a brackish/salt concoction that affects current water supply plants that are not equipped with desalination processes. The sea-level changes also affect the water quality and may spur harmful algal blooms in conjunction with altering fish migration patterns, bringing potentially devastating effects to the commercial and recreational fishing industry.

Global climate change can also affect the way that rain falls and where it goes. Drought patterns are affected by localized or regional climate patterns such as El Niño, but global climate change has the potential to alter those rain patterns fundamentally and to make the change permanent. And although drought may take hold of a region for a couple of years, parching the land, it can be followed by torrential rain patterns that wipe the arid ground clean of topsoil and cause other effects, such as flooding, landslides, and destruction of property. The Southeast United States has been in the grip of a drought that is continuing through the writing of this book, although recent rain patterns have returned to a normal wet season total. Still, it will take a long time to recover from the drought. This is happening worldwide. The vast plains of Africa are being affected by a worsening drought situation. The Sahara desert is expanding, and rain is not falling with the frequency that it did in the past. Rainfall pattern changes have grave implications for agricultural production. To be sure, the rain has to fall somewhere, but the vast swaths of productive farmland today may not be usable in the coming decades, as the shifting rain patterns change the game. This is especially an issue in many parts of the world for sustenance farmers who rely on small farming to provide food for their families and the local village.

Rainfall patterns also affect potable water supplies. Clean drinking water is now an all-too-precious commodity for many parts of the world. Contaminated drinking water causes disease and death for millions of Third World citizens. In parts of Southeast Asia and Africa, drinking water supplies have been linked to serious disease outbreaks. And, in many cases, children are the most affected. Getting drinking water to these regions is difficult enough, but if rainfall patterns change and make areas that have barely any water now into areas that are completely devoid of a water supply, the potential ramifications can cause not only additional ecological problems but political ones as well.

The idea of environmental refugees is a new concept. In the past, refugees were usually displaced by war, famine, or natural disasters. The displacement of peoples has usually caused a host of problems, including ethnic tensions, civil war, and spikes in crime—against as well as by the refugees. It's never a good situation, and it is becoming more and more prevalent. A subgroup of environmental refugees, climate refugees, as they are now referred to, are people who are forced out of their lands by environmental changes brought about by climate changes and other long-term environmental issues. The United Nations predicts that in a few years there can be upward of 50 million people displaced by climate change disruptions. The first major move of a group of people as a result of rising sea levels was in Papua New Guinea, at the Carteret Atoll. The rising sea level was causing ecological problems, including wiping out food sources. Leaders told the media that "people are dying of starvation because salt-invaded gardens have failed."[4] Nearby island nations are also facing the same issues of rising sea levels and may be planning for mass immigration to Australia and New Zealand to avoid waiting too long for the sea level to claim their homes.

But environmental refugees don't always have to be large groups of indigenous peoples from Third World countries. Even in the United States there are small swaths of populations that have been forced out of their homes by environmental problems. Most of these are related to chemical spills, nuclear accidents, and long-term pollution of the groundwater and soil from industrial activities. There have been coal-mining disasters, such as the coal ash spills in Tennessee, and illegal dumping of toxic waste in poor, minority neighborhoods that have left big chunks of towns unfit for habitation. The one advantage in the United States is that we have the economic means and technological knowledge to work on these problems and address them; oftentimes this approach allows people to move back into the areas. There are federal and state brownfield programs that are set up specifically to rehabilitate formerly polluted areas and turn them into developable parcels of land for commercial and industrial uses. In some cases, they can also be used for residential purposes, depending on the severity of the pollution issue and the amount of clean up that has been done. There are buildings and park facilities on old landfills. The Tampa Bay Rays major league baseball team has considered an old landfill spot to build a potential future stadium. There are brownfield programs that work in conjunction with green developers and builders to restore blighted areas and make them models for sustainable redevelopment in urban cores.

Water pollution is a fact of life in many countries around the world. Even in the United States, where point source pollution has been severely curtailed by the Clean Water Act and a host of subsequent federal and state regulations, there are still water-quality problems in lakes, rivers, streams, and major saltwater bodies. Most of the pollution is no longer a result of chemicals being spewed out of massive pipes from smoke-belching factories. Rather, these days, it's non–point source pollution that is causing the greatest problems.

Atmospheric deposition rains down particulate matter—not only from places in the United States, but from foreign countries as well. Studies at the University of South Florida in St. Petersburg found that Saharan-borne dust from Africa got swept up in wind currents and dropped down thousands of miles away on the eastern seaboard of the United States. The implications are far-reaching for health and ecological reasons. The wind swept up dust that was created by climate changes and by the expansion of the Saharan desert. Coal-fired power plants are depositing mercury into the aquatic environment, where it is entering the food production system. Apex predators, such as sharks, swordfish, king mackerel, tuna, and other habitants of the ocean, have been found with high concentrations of mercury in their soft tissue. Again, it's a pollution concern that has public health implications. Many states have mercury advisories against eating large amounts of certain fish, especially for pregnant women. And do not think that you are off the hook because you live near a lake. High levels of mercury have been found in the muscle tissue of largemouth bass.

Stormwater runoff, discussed in a later chapter, is another water pollution issue. Excessive amounts of fertilizer from residential applications and agricultural uses have been in the news the last few years in relation to the massive Gulf of Mexico dead zone, located near the mouth of the Mississippi River. The dead zone has been appearing with regularity every year, and it is believed that the massive amount of nutrients running down the Mississippi—from agricultural operations and the residential developments along the river—are causing massive algae blooms, starving the water of oxygen, and leaving it an anaerobic mess. Divers with cameras have found no life present.

A similar event happened a couple years ago off the Gulf Coast of Florida. On the Atlantic Coast, there have been water pollution issues with regard to large-scale livestock operations, especially pig farms. There was a theory that the releases of high-nutrient concentrated slop water from the pig farms contributed to the massive *Pfiesteria* outbreak that killed thousands of fish and affected fishermen in the Carolinas and Virginia.

In addition to these agricultural runoff issues, general fertilizer plumes alone, from residential developments in cities along the water, have resulted in degraded water-quality indexes for many formerly pristine bodies of water. Even some remote lakes, because of the very size of their contributing watershed, have been negatively affected by runoff that has its origins hundreds of miles away. Even with increasingly stringent federal regulations, the waters of the United States can be helped by a green economy.

There are companies now that are leading the charge to address these environmental issues. In the water-resource area, there are pollution abatement technologies that are working for contaminated drinking water and surface water systems. There are many former chemical plants and industrial facilities that leeched various toxic chemicals into the ground, which have made their way into the water table. Often, by the time that these plumes are detected, they have been around for many years and can cause a variety of health issues. In some places, there has been evidence of cancer clusters, such as the recently discovered incidence of male breast cancer for people who grew up on the U.S. Marine base, Camp Lejeune. Also, there are pollutants that leech into surface water bodies, affecting fish and inveterate populations. In many bays and rivers, shellfishing is banned because the levels of pollutants are high and the mollusks filter-feeding causes them to store large amounts of the pollutants in their meat. That's one of the reasons that raw oysters and clams are usually flushed out at approved clean water facilities before being shipped to market. Again, it is often technology that is needed to remedy the situation, making things more habitable for people and less toxic for the environment.

With all that background and gloom-and-doom scenarios, it's clear why there is a real need for a change in the way we view not only our environment but our economy. In his book, Thomas Friedman called for a new space race (hence the name of this chapter) and outlined a general plan for breaking out of fossil fuel dependence and bringing about a paradigm shift to a more sustainable world. Friedman is also a keen political observer and knows that lessening dependence on foreign oil is a smart geopolitical move for the United States. Friedman's vision, as well as the vision of thousands of sustainability professionals, looks to the green collar business model as an economic driving force for even greater prosperity. And in that goal of greater prosperity comes a real ability to make employment opportunities available for people who may find themselves shut out of the new paradigm of science-based careers or for people who see a change in the way that their industry is headed.

It is imperative that the leadership of this shift to a green economy come from both the top and the bottom. It is the government that needs to set the leadership pace and take the country from where it is now to where it needs to go in the green economy. Inevitably, there will be stops along the way. There are lawmakers who don't see any benefit from environmentally sustainable practices and anti-science activists who want nothing more than to see science purged from the classroom, but their voices are being drowned out by the voices of common sense and knowledge of the issues and the industries. At the bottom, the consumers and job seekers have the most important position: they need to demand change from their representatives. But they also need to make the choices in the marketplace to cultivate and sustain companies willing to make a difference by offering goods and services that are along the lines of the green economy.

Making these choices sustainable may not always be the most cost-effective at first, but if enough people make them, the competition grows and the whole country gets lifted up with the wider variety of choices and positive economic benefit. And to be honest, cheap is good sometimes, but more often than not you get what you pay for. If you pay $1 more per pound for locally grown organic strawberries, you're getting a better product than berries that were shipped over 2,000 miles and are who-knows-how-old. By purchasing the local berries, you are also having a more positive effect on the local economy. Studies have found on average that up to three times as much money stays in the local community when you buy from a local business or farmer.

Proponents of a new green economy believe that the change to a more sustainable business model has far-reaching benefits, not only environmentally but economically. This green economy will mainly be fueled by renewable and alternative energies, as one of the cornerstones. It is believed that this change to a green economy "generates jobs, businesses and investments while expanding clean energy production, increasing energy efficiency, reducing greenhouse gas emissions, waste and pollution, and conserving water and other natural resources."[5] U.S. Labor Secretary Hilda Solis blogged, "Investments in the green economy can revitalize old industries, create new industries and generate new jobs for our workforce. These are jobs that will stay in the United States and cannot be outsourced. They will help pave a pathway out of poverty; strengthen urban and rural communities."[6]

Addressing the issues from both the environmental and economic benefit scenarios can work to sell the idea of a green economy to two oftentimes diametrically opposed groups: environmentalists and businessmen. To the environmentalists, a green economy attempts to address the ecological issues they care deeply about; to the businessmen, the same economy allows for innovation and a healthy bottom line while getting the marketing benefit of being green-conscious. It has the potential to be a win-win all around.

Sustainability is one the buzzwords of the new green mantra. The idea that we need to break our dependency on oil, use our natural resources wisely, watch our carbon footprint, reduce our waste and consumption, and improve environmental conditions is merging with the idea that these things can be done in conjunction with a wiser way to improve our economy, put people to work who have been shut out by outdated industries, enhance U.S. scientific acumen and technological leadership, and bring back a spirit of innovation.

The idea of a green collar economy fueled by green jobs has been taking hold on a national level. In 2007, President Bush signed the Green Jobs Act, which committed $125 million for green jobs training for veterans, displaced workers, and at-risk youth for jobs in "energy-efficient building, construction and retrofitting, renewable energy, energy-efficient vehicles, biofuels, and manufacturing of sustainable products using sustainable processes and materials."[7] The American Reinvestment and Recovery Act of 2009 is anticipated to rejuvenate the renewable energy industry, which has been hamstrung by weak credit markets and fluctuating energy prices, and double renewable output over the next three years. The Act provides over $500 million for green jobs training and the following monetary breakdown:

- $50 billion in energy efficiency efforts in schools, public buildings, and subsidized housing
- $18 billion for public transit projects
- $11 billion to modernize the electric grid and implement a smart grid

- $6 billion to accelerate environmental cleanup work in 12 states
- $5.9 billion in climate change and science research
- $2 billion for advanced battery manufacturing
- $1.6 billion in funds, grants, and tax credits for alternative-fuel vehicles
- $1.15 billion for job training in smart grid, energy efficiency, and other sectors[8]

To further illustrate how the federal government is viewing green jobs, in March of 2009, President Obama tapped green jobs activist Van Jones to be his advisor on green jobs. This was an historic event. It was the first time that there had been that kind of recognition at the national leadership level of the importance of the green economy. Van Jones is one of the top speakers on the subject of green jobs and works with disadvantaged and minority communities, helping them with training for green jobs. His belief, and one shared by the president, is that green jobs can aid these communities and bring them out of the economic malaise in which many of the residents feel trapped. By advancing the energy and environmental policies that the Obama administration is planning, Jones hoped to advance real green job creation. But, politics being the business it is, Van Jones stepped down from his post after some controversial statements and associations of his were brought out in the media. As of the time of the book's writing, no one has taken the position over. But the commitment is still there.

Though federal backing is just gearing up, at a more local level, environmental concerns have been at the forefront of policy for over a decade. More stringent federal regulations concerning topics from water pollution to land management have forced change on governments and businesses and, in turn, spawned an ever-increasing number of environmental professionals who are dedicated to assisting these entities with the latest laws. A lot of communities welcome the economic activity generated by green jobs, as well as by the use of sustainable methods for redevelopment of cities. Green has a cache for cities (the greenest city, etc.) from a marketing perspective, and areas of the country that rely on eco-tourism have a vested interest in keeping their environment as pristine as possible

There is also a parallel movement, mainly on the private side, that considers environmental sustainability as the driving force behind new business models and new careers. According to Ian Thompson, CEO and co-founder of CleanTechies, "Individual technological development will be driven by private ventures, while larger projects will be driven by government. When commercialization becomes viable, capitalism steps in."[9] Go to any trade show or conference in any environmental or engineering field and you'll see companies from around the country, and international to some extent, that are looking for ways to break into the larger sustainable products markets and to show off the innovation in manufacturing and design that is happening in small 1- to 10-employee shops in out of the way industrial parks.

Green has been a fad before. After the release of Al Gore's 1992 book, *Earth in the Balance*, the green movement seemed poised to explode on the scene, and to some extent it did. But it did not necessarily translate into a major new way of living. This time it seems different. There seems to be a real paradigm shift, and formerly disparate forces, such as sustainability and capitalism, are combining in a new kind of matrix. Says Will Duggan, a blogger on sustainability issues, "Sustainability isn't a nook or a cranny; it's the whole muffin and the butter too."[10]

The major difference between the green movement of 15 years ago and the one going on now is jobs: there are more jobs than ever in the green field. Coupled with an aging engineering and scientific workforce, the time is ripe for a major increase in opportunities for those seeking a career, whether their first or their fifth. And, unlike some other job categories, green careers range from blue collar factory jobs to high-level engineering jobs in high-tech labs.

CHAPTER 2

THE BASICS

So, the basics. To get green jobs, you first have to understand what they are, where they are located, where the training opportunities are, and where you can find available positions. It's like finding any other job or career, but, with all the information that's flying through the news sources, blogosphere, and Web, it's easy to get lost in the maze of conflicting reports and information. Green jobs are, for the most part, ones that either did not exist a short time ago or that are undergoing a metamorphosis from traditional blue collar occupations to new green collar versions. And these jobs can show up in the most unexpected places, and from the most unexpected sources.

The first question to ask is "What exactly is a green collar job?" Phil Angelides, of the Apollo Alliance, was quoted in a *Time* magazine article describing green collar jobs as "part of a real career path, with upward mobility. And it needs to reduce waste and pollution and benefit the environment."[1] Carl Pope, from the Sierra Club, told *The New York Times* that "A green job has to do something useful for people, and it has to be helpful to, or at least not damaging to, the environment."[2] Some aren't even sure how to quantify them. "The fact is, we don't really know what a green job is, let alone how to count them and measure their growth. In some cases, a new green job isn't even a new job but rather a 'retained' job — one that might have otherwise disappeared if not for its greenness."[3]

For the purposes of this book, the term *green* is used to describe careers that transcend the general environmental sciences, to encompass

nontraditional jobs that promote sustainability, as well as jobs in old industries that are adapting to the trend of sustainability. These are indicative of
the emergence of whole new classes of career tracks, utilizing pieces of
various disciplines and science. The basics are covered: alternative energy,
green building, and green marketing, along with some niche careers, such
as green journalism. You'll read about things that a few years ago just
didn't exist—green interior designers, wind turbine installation degrees,
and training programs for disadvantaged youths to become solar-panel
maintenance workers. By all means, the list is probably not complete. By
the time this book is one year old, there may be whole new categories of
green jobs. That's one of the exciting aspects of this field; the changes in
job descriptions are driven by the ever-increasing advances in scientific
understanding of environmental concerns.

The Foundation

Green jobs are most often associated with manufacturing-type jobs:
jobs that are supposed to bring back the "Made in the USA" brand and
take back the empty, hulking behemoths of abandoned factories. Manufacturing used to be the cornerstone of the U.S. economy. But, as Bruce
Springsteen sang, "these jobs are going boys and they ain't coming back."
Government figures show a loss of over 3 million manufacturing jobs
from 2000 through 2006. With the collapse of the U.S. auto industry in
2008, the numbers are even greater through 2009. Manufacturers have
been flocking to lower-cost regions such as China and Eastern Europe.
Environmental regulations are also lax in those countries, but the price
for those jobs is an astounding rate of air pollution, water pollution, and
resultant health issues. Another factor in manufacturing job losses is the
increasing productivity and mechanization of many jobs. What used to
take 10 workers to accomplish may now only take a single worker to run
the machine or watch over the robot that welds, shapes, and cuts and that
can work 24/7.

In the United States, more and more purchased items are manufactured overseas, backed by what some see as unfair trade agreements.
There's certainly the populist outrage that cries for jobs to come back to
the United States, but instead of waiting for those jobs to come back, we
need to be thinking two steps ahead and create job opportunities here
that can't be moved overseas—or ones that complement the global marketplace and offer a niche service that a company in China or India could
use as readily as U.S. companies that outsource their call centers to
Bangalore. For trades people and for those who worked in factories

for years and suddenly found themselves out of a job, green jobs, at least
the trades and mechanical ones, may be one way to bring them back into
the workforce. Coupled with the higher-level technical jobs that the
green collar workforce needs, the green economy starts to take on a
weight that can't easily be pushed aside.

In the last few years, the media has been playing up the idea of green
jobs, with headlines promising the sky: Payscale.com asked, "Are Green
Careers the Next Google?"; Hugg.com wondered, "Can Green Save the
Faltering Middle Class?" Green jobs have gone from "What?" to "Oh, I
know, solar energy, wind power, fuel cells." But for all the new familiarity with the concept, most people still are unaware of how to train for
these positions or what they need to know to pull themselves up to the
table and get a chance to be part of the new economy.

The basic starting point of getting into a green job is the right kind
of training/education. It's impossible to parse out all the specific qualifi-
cations and qualities for individual green jobs. Many change across job
classifications, as well as across geographical regions. A green builder in
Minnesota has different challenges than a green builder in Florida. But
there are a few general skills that anyone looking to get into a green
career should have. Many green jobs are merely a furtherance of existing positions and skill sets, specifically among tradespeople such as electricians and construction workers. The skills needed for the basic job are
there. It's a matter of updating the skill set, through training, to conform
to changes such as new green building codes or to use electricity from
alternative energy such as solar. "The new energy economy will create
some brand new industries and many brand new jobs. But even more of
it will involve transforming the industries and jobs we already have."[4]

This is especially true for the more blue collar jobs that green has
crept into, areas such as construction, wind and solar parts manufacturing, green heating ventilation and cooling installation, green contract-
ing, etc. This is an area where government-sponsored green jobs
training programs really come through. It's far easier to train skilled
workers in updating their knowledge base than to train a person fresh off
the street. But the programs also look to put out-of-work citizens back
to work. In this case, some remedial back training may be needed. The
government-run training programs are often broad enough to give a
good base level of knowledge before going off to more specialized trainings. Especially when dealing with alternative energy, the book indicates
that community colleges offer certificate programs in jobs such as solar
panel installation. Some private companies even offer non–school-related
training certifications.

For some other career paths, a little training gets your foot in the door, and your continuing training and experience pave the way for future job growth and advancement. Positions such as wind turbine technician or solar panel installer need more formalized training than just the basic background experience in a trade and then learning on the job. It's these jobs that many green collar training programs at state and local levels are targeting. These middle sector jobs are the ones with the potential for real growth.

For more specialized green careers, higher education is key, at least a 4-year degree to get into a position and either additional education or experience to move ahead. Some add-on specialties, such as environmental law, are already part of the curriculum for students in the program. Engineering is another growth field that needs qualified personnel with, at the least, a bachelor's degree and the ability to get a professional engineer's license.

Computer skills are usually a given. In the rapidly changing technological landscape, keeping up computer skills on a regular basis is even more essential than ever. Many companies offer in-house trainings or pay for employees to train on the latest software that is germane to their particular job. Even that may not be enough. Employees and job seekers need to expand their skill set to stay ahead of the curve. It reaps rewards down the line, from higher pay to more advancement potential. It's never too late to start learning a new skill or to brush up on ones that you haven't used in a while.

Computer software ranges across the various career paths and job sets, but basic word processing and spreadsheet software knowledge is a good foundation. Some jobs require Geographic Information System (GIS) skills, whereas others ask for modeling, which in itself encompasses hundreds of computer programs—modeling everything from climate change to water levels to water quality. The easiest way to get a sense of what types of computer skills you'll need is to look at specific job descriptions in the areas that interest you. In some of the Resources sections in this and other chapters, we'll give some leads to where to look for computer classes that are specific for job groups.

Skill in mechanics is needed for the more traditional manufacturing jobs that are now going green. But even then, they often need to be coupled with a familiarity for new technology and some computer knowledge. The one good thing about the manufacturing industry is the learn-on-the-job aspect. Actually working on an assembly line at a wind turbine factory can give you more job knowledge at times than reading about it in a book or taking a class.

Networking is a part of any career path, from jobs in the trades to high-level scientific careers. Each specific type of job, especially in the sciences, often has multiple associations, which in turn hold conferences and trade shows. In addition to being great places to catch up on the latest technology and to find out advances in the field, they are also the very best places to mingle with other experts in the field, as well as matching people with potential new job positions and, additionally, making contacts that can bring new clients to private companies, whether consultants or seller of a particular product.

What Are Green Jobs?

What kind of jobs are categorized as being green? There are wide varieties, and the categories are expanding almost daily. Many of the major job categories that other industries have can all fall under green jobs. Throughout the book, as various areas of environmental issues are examined, jobs specific to those areas (e.g., wind turbine manufacturer, green product marketer, etc.) are featured.

But for all the specifics, there are some jobs that are almost universally green jobs. Environmental scientists, by the very nature of their work, whether working for public agencies, private companies, universities, or nonprofits and NGOs, are working in a green career field. Environmental science is quickly becoming one of the more popular science majors at colleges and universities. At my alma mater, Eckerd College in St. Petersburg, Florida, the environmental science major started with a handful of graduates in 1994. It's now supplanting the traditional popular major, marine science.

Jobs will come from traditional career tracks, such as engineering and science, ones that really don't need much a shift to be green collar careers. They are ones that are also seeing an increase in demand, coupled with the so-called old man syndrome. At any engineering conference, there is a majority of people within 10 years of retirement with an age gap behind them. The Bureau of Labor Statistics reports that "by 2014, there will be 31.2 percent more jobs for environmental engineers than there were in 2004."[5] Schools around the country have begun to address this shortcoming by stressing science and technology in STEM programs (Science, Technology, Engineering, and Math).

Similar predictions are in for solar panel installers, wind turbine designers, water-resource engineers, green architects, landscape architects, and environmental lawyers. The world of green is showing up in boardrooms of financial companies and of mutual funds that invest in cutting-edge technology.

Who Is Hiring?

What kind of companies and agencies are hiring green workers? Well, technically everyone. Green jobs are in private industry, public agencies, and NGOs. But let's get a little more specific.

Private companies that are looking for green jobs start with alternative and traditional energy companies. These corporations are looking for ways to expand production and use of green technology. From small upstarts making wind turbines to British Petroleum (BP), the green paradigm is an increasingly larger share of the energy pie. In rational energy companies, environmental concerns have come a long way since the *Exxon Valdez* disaster. In fact, most of the companies now have sustainability officers. BP has been one of the traditional energy companies that have made the big push into renewables. Under the banner of BP Alternative, the company has "invested around $2.9 billion in wind, solar, biofuels, and hydrogen power"[6] since 2005. Other traditional energy corporations are aggressively pursuing not only the big alternative energy but increasing development of natural gas refineries, moving into the oil sands of Canada, and looking to make clean coal a cornerstone of power stations.

Environmental consulting companies are another big employer for green jobs. These firms have been around for decades under the usual environmental services, but some are now moving into alternative energy audits, compliance with cap-and-trade regulations, low-impact development, and green building. As we go through the chapters and other job areas, you will see some of the types of companies that are employing green job seekers.

Environmental activist groups and other NGOs are also major employers of green job seekers. Most of these jobs, realistically, do not pay as well as those in private companies, nor do they always pay as well as the public sector. Benefits are sometimes nonexistent. The trade-off is a sense of purpose and a real reward, namely that you are making a difference in the environment. These activist organizations include small regional groups that are bound together to address small local environmental issues. That dirty creek or trash-clogged estuary is often the impetus for some of these smaller organizations. Although a few of these disappear over time, some expand to larger issues and can join with major national organizations. These groups generally like employees with a degree in environmental science and a flair for public outreach and political activism. Others, especially groups that concentrate on restoration activities, look for people with broad science backgrounds, who are BASS ready to get down and dirty in the muck and woods, cutting down invasive species, counting wildlife, planting native trees, etc.

National NGOs, such as the Sierra Club or the Nature Conservancy, are another option. These organizations rely mainly on volunteers and could be a great place for college students to intern. These organizations can also be international in scope and can offer a chance to do some environmental work overseas. But, like the local NGOs, the jobs that come with these groups can pay less. Of course, there's always the fact that people view green jobs as a rewarding career option and don't care as much about the financial aspect of it.

The public sector is usually characterized as a more stable work environment. And although public agencies can be a little stingy pay-wise, the benefits are usually top-notch, coupled with a pension plan. This can have unintended consequences. Many senior-level staff get into their position and stay there ... for a long time. In some agencies, this can stymie growth opportunities for lower-level employees. It's a common problem in many public departments.

The most common public agencies to look for green jobs include public works and local environmental departments. It's where I got my start working in water-quality and stormwater permitting. These jobs offer a wealth of varied experience. Unlike working with private companies, job classifications allow for wide latitude in work projects. While working at the county, I was involved with freshwater and saltwater fish surveys, sea grass monitoring, water-quality sampling, lake management, watershed management, benthic sampling, industrial inspections, illicit discharge inspections, levying fines for stormwater ordinance violations, and public outreach. It's a way to gain experience and build your résumé that narrowly focused jobs can't give you.

Many local governments are looking at low-impact development ordinances and green building as ways to spur local economic development and to revive older urban cores. For planners, environmental engineers, and green building professionals, there are job opportunities there. Counties are also looking at sustainability issues and always need people who can advise them on ways to reduce operating expenses. I've seen job listings for sustainability officers and advisors for municipalities across the United States and Canada on many of the job board sites. Biologists, alternative energy specialists, civil engineers, green marketers, and environmental scientists are all sought after for local government positions.

At the national level, the federal agencies that green job seekers should look into include the Environmental Protection Agency (EPA); Department of the Interior (DOI); National Oceanographic and Atmospheric Administration (NOAA), which also includes the National Marine Fisheries Service); United States Fish and Wildlife Service; and National Institute of Health. The federal government also has a host of research laboratories affiliated with these agencies and with local universities. Positions with the federal government include all levels of scientists and engineers—from water resources to air quality to biology to biotechnology. The federal agencies also hire tradespeople such as mechanics, builders, and Heating, Ventilating, and Air Conditioning (HVAC) professionals. Federal work can be fairly stable and pay well, not to mention the federal benefits package, which is generally competitive, if not better, than that of some private companies.

Where the Jobs Are

It's easy to say that the jobs are everywhere. As of 2008, 46 states provided some types of tax incentives for renewable energy or green job training programs. The notion of a clean, green economy is an idea that has permeated almost every sector of government, from national down to small municipalities. Even though it seems that you could be anywhere in the country and get a green job, in fact there are specific areas of the country that favor certain green jobs over others. You'll find green marketing jobs in larger urban environments and manufacturing jobs mainly across the Midwest and Great Plains. But at the heart of finding where the jobs are is not just knowing which states and regions are making the effort to lure green jobs to their locales, but who is spending the money to train workers.

With the tight economic conditions at the time of the writing of this book, it's difficult to forecast how states that have used public money to finance training and investment in clean energy and green jobs will cope with reductions in budgets as a result of the recession. Some have stated their willingness to keep the funding alive; other states are looking for more private investment and venture capital. It's never easy for states coping with dwindling tax revenues to suggest raising taxes for anything, but if the promise of green jobs from government investment holds true at least partially, selling the idea will be easier down the line. As you will see later, in a chapter on green marketing, selling the idea of green is in itself a viable career option for the eco-minded.

At the national level, there is a sudden increase in visibility with regard to green jobs. With the recent stimulus funding and assorted energy bills, the federal government has taken some baby steps toward cultivating a greener economic climate. It's hoped that these funds will not only create jobs directly but also encourage private investment. There is a leadership push in Washington to reduce greenhouse gas emissions significantly and to improve engine efficiency for all new cars, in addition to changing emission standards. These rules will be part of the regulatory framework that drives the innovation of companies looking to get their green products to the marketplace.

But the real changes are being made at the state and local levels. They have followed the federal government's lead and, in many cases, have taken far bolder steps to embrace what many political leaders see as a real paradigm shift in the future economic development of their respective regions. In many states, the departments of environmental protection already implement many of the federal environmental mandates, as well as enforce their own regulations and programs. These programs can promote the idea of sustainability in energy efficiency and usage, green job training, and outreach designed to go out into the communities where unemployment is high and educate citizens about green jobs. The job programs are run by a number of existing agencies, and a few states have made green training a cornerstone of new departments. Green building is another area where local and state governments have taken a good lead in implementing green ideas and turning them into reality. State departments of transportation are taking green building ideas to road projects, through the use of different building materials, and designing drainage systems that help treat the runoff, rather than just sending it off the road and into the nearest body of water. Local governments are pushing for some of the building projects that they fund to be green-certified and looking at development plans such as new urbanism for use in redevelopment master plans.

At the state level, tax incentives and rebate programs have traditionally been the mechanism of influence for green energy and efficiency standards. But states are now going further, even pushing their own green programs onto their citizens. Close to 30 states have mandates about the amount of clean energy that power companies and utilities must provide. Other states have laws limiting pollutant discharges from power generation facilities. Another major effort that was virtually unknown even a couple years ago is the large number of direct green jobs training programs that states are advocating, especially after the start of the latest recession in 2007.

In New England, Governor Deval Patrick of Massachusetts, as part of his Pathways out of Poverty program, dedicated over $1 million for green training, specifically aimed for depressed cities such as Brockton and Worcester, former industrial cities, now coping with the new labor outlook. The state legislature also passed an investment in clean energy act, which has shown dividends—as alternative energy companies have begun to either relocate to Massachusetts or stay in the state, despite efforts from other locales to lure them away with financial incentives. Governor Patrick's overtures to private companies have also shown results.

Other New England states have shown some promise in green careers, although Vermont was recently cited by a report as lagging behind the rest of New England in green job creation. By 2008, Rhode Island had attracted over $22 million in venture capital private funding for its green jobs. There is also interest in building a field of wind turbines off the Rhode Island coast, spurred on by a private wind energy company. The company says that project alone would employ over 800 green collar workers.

In California, Governor Arnold Schwarzenegger announced the creation of California Green Corps, a program to steer at-risk young adults into green career paths and provide on-the-job and classroom training. Started in early 2009, the Green Corps is a $20 million pilot project, working with over 1,000 people, specializing in energy, computers, and general green worker skills. Los Angeles combated its rising unemployment numbers in 2009 by passing an innovative green jobs bill that would retrofit many of the city's municipal buildings.[7] The bill was passed with the help of the Apollo Alliance, a "coalition of labor, business, environmental, and community leaders working to catalyze a clean energy revolution that will put millions of Americans to work in a new generation of high-quality, green-collar jobs."[8] California got some good news in mid-2009, when a study showed that California "created the most green jobs: 125,390 . . . Pay scales among the new jobs ranged from $21,000 to $111,000 a year."[9]

New Jersey has instituted a variety of programs and legislation aimed at green jobs and economic improvement. Through federal grants, close to 2,000 workers have been trained under the Green Job Training Partnership Programs. A private energy company recently gave the training program a grant for $300,000. Another step that is being taken at the legislative level in New Jersey is the Energy Savings Improvement legislation, designed to encourage millions in private investment to state universities, schools, and municipalities lowering energy usage and creating green jobs. Coupled with the governor's program to increase energy efficiency and invest in new energy technologies, the energy-driven programs are expected to create over 3,000 jobs in 1 year. New Jersey's governor's office also estimates that investment in alternative energy in New Jersey can create over 20,000 jobs between 2009 and 2020.

The nation's largest city, New York City, is probably not what most people think of when it comes to an ideal green environment for living. In fact, as an aside, studies have shown that city dwellers are far more energy-efficient than suburban or rural residents. Most of that is related to carbon footprint reduction, from using mass transit and eschewing cars, but water and energy efficiency are also higher. Manhattan has one of the lowest comparable water usage rates in the country. So a major environmental initiative announced by the city was not entirely unexpected. Announced in 2007, "plaNYC" is a visionary program from Mayor Michael Bloomberg to green the country's largest city and to make green jobs one of the centerpieces of the city's economy. The plan is specifically designed to reduce the city's carbon footprint while accommodating an anticipated increase in population of 1 million residents. New York City, as a global business and financial center, has a myriad of opportunities for green collar careers. However, there are some drawbacks, namely the cost of living, which can be a barrier when dealing with lower-level positions.

The Great Plains states have been hit by a brain drain over the last few decades and, in some areas, are experiencing large population losses as young people and workers move elsewhere to find jobs. But the trend has been slowing, as old manufacturing facilities have been brought to life again by green companies. In Grand Forks, North Dakota, Danish wind turbine company LM Glasfibre has a manufacturing plant. The small town of Minster, Ohio, has gotten in on the renewable energy track with Minster Machine Company, which is making cast iron parts for wind turbines and was recently profiled on CNN.com. But even with all the anecdotal stories about green jobs in the Rust Belt, it's difficult to know exactly what impact green jobs are having. According to a CNN reporter, "Scores of firms in the renewable energy business have recently opened in the Rust Belt states. They hope to take advantage of a population known for its industrial skills, engineering ability and work ethic. It's hard to say how many people these firms currently employ. The government doesn't yet track green jobs and the distinction between what's 'green' and what isn't often gets blurred."[10]

With the demise of the U.S. automobile industry, Michigan has been one of the hardest hit states, in terms of reduction in workforce and number of companies that were severely cutting back or going out of business altogether. At the time of the writing of this book, in June 2009,

Michigan's unemployment rate was above 12 percent, above the national average. There have been some calls for an economic overhaul of the state's manufacturing base. Firms have complied to some extent. There were over 350 firms in green business-related ventures in the state, including some wind turbine manufacturing facilities. But it hasn't been enough to stem the tide of rising unemployment and a sense of despair overtaking the former manufacturing giant. Even if the current U.S. auto crisis maintains its pace or gets slightly better, there aren't going to be enough jobs to bring back the laid-off workers. Instead, the state government has proposed a No Worker Left Behind strategy. The program is designed to give out-of-work Michigan residents "two years worth of free tuition at any community college, university, or other approved training provider to gain the skills and credentials for new careers in high-demand occupations, emerging industries, or to start a business."[11]

The Pacific Northwest is an area of the country that has been lauded for its progressive ideas and practices when it comes to the environment and sustainability. Oregon, hit hard by the 2008–2009 recession, passed a green jobs training bill in the summer of 2009, with the intent of bringing additional green jobs to the state. Oregon was one of the states identified in a Pew study as having a growth in green jobs, even during the low point of the recession. The Northwest's ethos of sustainable living is a perfect place to start a green job as well. Many small environmental firms and energy companies started in the Pacific Northwest. It's certainly one of the areas that a job seeker should look at.

Nevada has an aggressive program to bring solar power to government buildings, schools, and residential neighborhoods. As a result, when it comes to alterative energy jobs, Nevada had one of the strongest growths during the 2000s, over 25 percent. For a state that was hit hard by the declining real estate market, the Nevada growth in green jobs was a bright spot in the local economy.

South Carolina reported close to 12,000 employees in the clean energy sector in 2007, and that number was expected to grow, although the recession tapered off all employment figures. Companies in South Carolina are involved in solar technology, biofuels, and other alternative energy products. North Carolina is in an even better position because of the research triangle area, which already houses a large number of science-based businesses and academic institutions. North Carolina's green jobs are more spread out across various job sectors, including green building, green development, and biotechnology.

Florida grew its green collar jobs, spurred mainly by clean energy positions, by 7.9 percent between 1998 and 2007. Much of the growth was organic, but there was a shot in the arm brought about by Governor Charlie Crist's environmental policies. The governor signed laws strengthening the state's dedication to alternative energy and instituting one of the first state-sponsored cap-and-trade programs for emissions. Florida is also buoyed by a strong scientific community that is dedicated to water resources, from both engineering and biological research perspectives. Like California, Florida's large coastline is a major economic engine that feeds tourism, the largest industry in the state. By being at the cutting edge of water-quality improvement technology and innovation, Florida has improved its water, maintaining the tourist base so vital for its economic well-being.

Texas already has a significant wind power industry; it is the largest producer of wind energy in the country and is planning on adding more capacity and production turbines to its arsenal. And state lawmakers believe that "Texas is uniquely positioned to lead the way to green jobs and clean power."[12] Texas has instituted its own green jobs development program and has tax incentives for other green initiatives. Cities such as Austin have convened their own green jobs task forces, many through their local chambers of commerce. For a state that is so known for its petroleum resources and traditional energy companies, the amount of work that is being done to embrace the emergence of a green economy demonstrates a significant change: the sense that an oil-based future is not certain is shared even in the heart of oil country.

Not all states are created equal. There are still swaths of the Great Plains and states such as West Virginia that are behind the curve when it comes to green job creation. Even in states where green jobs programs have already begun, there is improvement needed in some of the training programs and the economic oversight of running the programs. Also, some states hit hard by the recession have cut back on funding, which could be detrimental to their recovery if they are serious about adding green careers as the cornerstone of their economy. But even with these setbacks, the trailblazers have set a path that the local and state government can follow to set up green job training programs and give tax incentives and other enticements for upstart businesses to incubate and prosper. The mechanisms are coming into place; the next step is for the leaders to take that step.

Many of the anticipated manufacturing jobs are not going to be in the large, idle GM factories, or fit the stereotypical idea of large-scale manufacturing companies sprawled over acres. Instead, smaller companies and light manufacturing will help fill the niche. These nimbler companies are better structured to serve as the interface between innovation and commercialization in the marketplace. And these smaller companies are usually incubators for engineers and scientists who are unencumbered by excessive corporate governance. The other advantage for many of these smaller companies and upstarts is geographical needs. They are far more able to move headquarters to emerging markets if needed, or to have a smaller physical presence, enhancing their flexibility and ultimately their competitiveness in the new global marketplace.

How Much?

The first question for any job seeker is usually, "How much does the job pay?" It's a logical question and one that can't be readily answered across the board for green jobs. It's difficult to give accurate numbers for jobs that are so new in their creation. However, there are some data to let job seekers at least know what type of position would fit their interest and salary goals.

Not every green job is a money-making machine. Jobs in "recycling processing pay as low as $8.25 an hour and jobs in renewable energy manufacturing facilities pay as little as $11 an hour."[13] A survey of manufacturers of wind and solar products found that the wages were 10–20 percent less than the average manufacturing wages in the United States. However, that did not take into account the inclusion of high-paying auto workers. And, in some areas of the country dominated by service and retail jobs, these manufacturing positions, even if the pay is fairly low, are better than many existing opportunities. Still, it's up to job seekers to find out as much as they can about the current wages being paid in certain manufacturing sector for jobs.

Even in the same industry, such as solar, although an assembly line worker in a manufacturing plant may make only $14 per hour, a panel installer can make up to $75,000 per year, depending on the usual factors of experience, location, and demand. The same is true in the wind industry. Green builders pay a day laborer far less than a specialized HVAC guy who works with updated green systems. It's the same as in most other areas of the economy: the higher the skill set, the better chance for a higher paycheck.

Salaries also increase exponentially with higher-level technical positions. Design engineers, sales managers, marketers, and so on have salaries that are above those in manufacturing, but some of the green industries, such as green building and water engineering, are finding themselves short of qualified people. The salaries reflect that. Chief technology officers for green companies can make over $100,000 per year.

Chief executives can make twice that. Research and development and design engineers can make over $100,000 per year. Architects specializing in green building can make over $100,000 per year as well.

Salary resources for individual green job sectors can be found by looking into trade organizations and national groups, such as the National Association of Environmental Professionals. Their Tampa, Florida, chapter puts out a salary matrix each year, showing the average salaries for a variety of environmental and engineering positions in the Tampa Bay region. Other chapters and associations have similar resources. And keep in mind that some areas of the country traditionally pay less, based on the cost of living and need for expertise.

The U.S. Bureau of Labor Statistics released some median annual salary figures in 2009: insulation worker, $30,800; recycling worker, $26,400; energy audit specialist, $40,300; environmental engineer, $76,000; environmental engineer technician, $42,800; microbiologist, $64,600; and physicist, $93,300.[14] The numbers vary widely, based on the level of expertise needed for the positions, but they give a fairly good overall range of salaries for some of the more common green careers.

Panacea or Hot Air?

Before we get farther into talking about the various job opportunities in green, it's worth discussing how realistic are the projections of 3, 4, or even 40 million green jobs created as a result of government and private investment in the field. In reality, it's always difficult to predict how a new type of career path will turn out. The same scenario could be applied to computer technology back in the 1970s, when it would have been unimaginable to predict how many jobs would be computer science-related.

One thing I did with everyone that I interviewed for this book, or asked about their opinions, was to see what they thought were green job categories that were overhyped or ones that may not pan out as much as the pundits say they will. With few exceptions, most interviewees were hard-pressed to think of specific green job categories that may not pan out as everyone hopes. Alternative energy expert John Merlino discussed jobs in hydrogen fuel-cell technology: "The hydrogen economy may not happen quickly due to our bad economy and lower fossil energy costs. If government funding promoted hydrogen generation, distribution, storage, and fuel-cell technologies, then progress will happen faster."[15]

A recent academic study found that "green jobs estimates include huge numbers of clerical, bureaucratic, and administrative positions that do not produce goods and services for consumption."[16] The study looked through various green jobs reports from the mainstream media, as well as specialty organizations, and found no way to estimate accurately exactly how many green jobs would be created. It further argued against government subsidies of certain green technologies. Although this may strike some as being biased in favor of a complete free-market approach to green job creation, it does bring up a lot of cautionary flags.

Another recent study, in Spain, caused some ripples when noted columnist George Will used it as the basis for his weekly op/ed column, basically trying to say that green jobs would destroy more jobs that they create. The study was based on how Spain went about investing in clean energy and how that affected associated traditional energy positions and the overall unemployment figure. There have been rebuttals to the study in the way it was done and some of the assumptions made. Also, it should be kept in mind that the study was specific to Spain and really cannot be used to quantify how similar situations would occur in the United States.

In April 2009, Missouri Senator Kit Bond announced a report from his subcommittee on green jobs entitled "Yellow Lights for Green Jobs," which gave a hard look at the cost of green jobs versus tax subsidies, as well as average wages of green jobs, and whether the hype of the number of jobs created is equal to the real numbers. Even though the report was criticized for its approach by some green job activists and other academic studies on green jobs, it did reveal that a cautionary approach might work best for some sectors of the new green economy. And the report didn't sound the death knell for green job creation, but rather suggested a closer look at how government investment in green jobs is done. In reality, any critiques of the current green jobs incentive program can only make it more effective and allow private investment to work itself into the mix.

President Obama's former green jobs czar, Van Jones, was also asked point-blank if green jobs were overhyped. Jones stated that, although the idea that every American is going to have a green job tomorrow is definitely overhyped, the green jobs movement is so young that it's impossible to predict how long it will take to come to fruition. "The civil rights movement took several decades. The women's rights movement took several decades. Other environmental movements are taking several decades. We need to give the green-jobs movement at least a chance to turn green before we declare it dead."[17]

Regardless of how you view the studies, it's always essential to keep a clear head and look beyond the hype and inflated numbers of jobs created. Green jobs are like any other new idea. There is always a certain

Amount of inflated expectations. And although proponents are quick to jump on those numbers, opponents are quick to dismiss the impact of green jobs if they don't equate with the predictions. It's a tightrope walk, to be sure. However, as you'll see throughout this book, there are real opportunities in real career paths with real prospects for a future. A little legwork and a realistic expectation of the kind of salary and longevity are needed to be successful.

Education/Training

General environmental educational programs are found throughout higher education institutions across the country. Prospective students should look through the individual course offerings and choose a program that concentrates on the environmental areas they want to study but that will also offer them the greatest opportunity for a long-term career. In later chapters, which focus on specific green job sectors, there is a listing of colleges and universities that offer programs in those areas. For a general environmental degree, the following resources are listed.

Training programs have been the favorite way to push the concept of green jobs into low-income and disadvantaged areas as a means for residents to rise out of poverty. But these programs are also useful for displaced workers, especially in manufacturing. In fact, as of mid-2009, "about $150 million in grants are earmarked for green job training programs that provide 'pathways out of poverty,' and a portion of some $290 million in grants will go toward efforts to retrain workers from the hard-hit auto industry."[18]

Another way—not so much formal training, but a way to get the experience needed for advancement in the field and for college students as a way to pad their résumés for their first career job—is to volunteer for environmental NGOs or to seek internships with public agencies or in academia. Internships are especially rewarding. The old adage of the interns just being around to clean the floors and get coffee is not based on reality. Nowadays, interns work in the field, collect data, assist with reports, and, yes, still do some of the grunt work. But there is more of a real push to mentor and train interns in environmental positions. Volunteers generally spend less time with the respective agency or company, but they do get their foot in the door and make excellent networking contacts. Either way is a smart idea for someone looking to get into the green career field.

In the following list are resources for new job seekers and those looking to make a change in career path. The list of training programs is just a small taste of the vast number of federal, state, and local programs, not to mention the huge variety of private training institutes and certification programs. Some of the latter chapters have specified training resources for the career path. It's worthwhile to start looking first at the local level with municipal governments, then to the state for any recent job training programs that are offered, many free of charge. As the green job genre matures, training programs will change and expand. Some of these sites will help you keep track of changes in certifications and educational requirements for positions.

- Apollo Alliance (apolloalliance.org). The Apollo Alliance is probably the best known green jobs organization in the country. The Alliance works with business and governments to gain support for training programs, secure funding for green jobs programs—supporting government green job training efforts at the city level and working on public outreach to bring their message of a green-powered economy to the citizens. The Web site also has a lot of research and reading material for people interested in green jobs.
- Association for the Advancement of Sustainability in Higher Education (www.aashe.org). This group seeks to bring the message of sustainable education and practices to colleges and universities. The association also sponsors conferences, professional development workshops, and a reporting system for schools—and to their commitment not only to sustainability in the way in which they operate the schools, but to courses and curriculums integrating themes of environmental stewardship and sustainability.
- California Green Solutions (www.californiagreensolutions.com). California is one of the model states when it comes to green jobs, from Van Jones's work in the north to various neighborhood groups and workforce agencies in the south. This site is geared toward citizens rather than a technical audience and lists green job training programs, helpful green job hints, and it promotes green products and solutions to environmental issues at a local level.
- Employment and Training Administration(ETA)/United States Department of Labor (www.doleta.gov). With the recent stimulus legislation shelling out millions for green job training and creation, the ETA will be the agency that oversees the training programs, job placement, and other resources for displaced

worked or new job seekers. The ETA works through local and
state initiatives, not through the Department of Labor directly.

- Enviroeducation (www.enviroeducation.com/). A division of the
  powerful job search site Monster.com, Enviroeducation is a one-
  stop shop for schools across the country, Canada, and the United
  Kingdom that offer degrees in environmental studies, specialized
  environmental programs, and other green topics such as ecotourism. It's an easy-to-use site, with a vast trove of resources.
  You can search by city, state, type, and subject.
- Green Career Institute (www.greencollarschool). Located in
  California, the Institute offers training programs and certificates in solar cell design, solar design sales, and solar energy
  and technology.
- Green Energy Ohio (www.greenenergyohio.org). As a Rust
  Belt state, Ohio has embraced the potential of green jobs and
  renewable energy as a way to improve the state's economic situation. This site is a comprehensive source of information
  about the green economy of the Buckeye State. This organization holds training seminars and workshops across the state
  for solar energy, clean energy, and specific certifications for
  green jobs.
- International Brotherhood of Electrical Workers (IBEW)
  (www.ibew.org). Apart from the activist aspect of the IBEW, the
  union runs a series of green jobs training programs in various
  union halls around the country. The emphasis is on solar and
  wind energy, but the jobs also encompass areas of green design
  and building.
- LA Infrastructure and Sustainability Jobs Collaborative
  (www.lattc.edu). The Collaborative is a coalition of private and
  public interests stressing training and education for low-income
  populations in order to benefit from green energy companies
  and opportunities in the field.
- New Jersey Clean Energy Program (www.njcleanenergy.com).
  The New Jersey program offers day-long symposiums, technical
  courses, certificate trainings, grant assistance, job placement
  assistance, and conferences in clean energy topics. The training
  programs are offered around the state on a regular basis.
- New York City Green Jobs Training Programs (http://
  www.nyc.gov/html/planyc2030/html/training/training.shtml).
  Part of the Bloomberg plaNYC program, this resource site offers
  a list of over 40 green job training programs located in New

York City, from city-operated programs to ones offered by private organizations.

- Northwest Environmental Training Center (www.nwetc.org).
  The Center is based in Seattle and offers a wide range of environmental training programs for the United States and Canada.
  In addition to professional development, they offer classes in
  green jobs training, home energy audits, habitat restoration,
  and public outreach and education.
- Oakland Green Jobs Corps (www.ellabarkercenter.org/index
  .php?p=gcjc_greenjobs_corps). The Corps is probably the
  best-known green jobs training program in the country; it
  was also one of the first that Van Jones, the former green jobs
  czar in the Obama administration, helped develop the program with other agencies and people in the community. The
  program starts with a 16-week preparatory course to get students competent in basic construction and trades skills such
  as blueprint reading and safety issues. After that, the students
  begin a 12-week intensive course on solar energy, green construction, and energy efficiency. The first class of 42 students
  is anticipating carpenter, solar installer, and green construction jobs. The nonprofit is also expected to receive some additional federal funding to expand class enrollment.
- Regional Technical Training Center (www.rttc.us). Based in
  California, the Center offers training in environmental engineering, solar energy, hazardous waste management, and
  biotech. It works directly with industrial leaders to tailor each
  training course for specific skills that companies are looking for
  or are lacking in current employees.
- Slippery Rock University of Pennsylvania/MS in Sustainability
  (http://www.sru.edu/). This is an example of a degree program
  suited for the new green collar economy. The program at Slippery Rock is an integrated program that combines natural
  resources management, sustainable agriculture, design of systems, and energy production. The sustainability degree is
  offered through the school's Alternative Living Technology and
  energy Research Project.
- Veterans Green Jobs (www.veteransgreenjobs.org). A group
  dedicated to finding U.S. veterans jobs in the green field, this
  training academy offers courses in energy efficiency and conservation, biofuels, green building and historic building preservation, natural resources conservation, and disaster response.

The site also links to green job resources and assists graduates of the course with placement.

Job Resources

It might seem like the usual step after the education and training is the job search. Actually, though, it's better to look at what jobs are available and what geographical locations seem to be attracting certain job types. The thought of picking up and moving halfway around the country might not be palatable for everyone, but for someone just out of college or looking to make a change, moving to where certain types of environmental careers are clustered can bring you to the opportunities.

As with any source for employment, job-posting Web sites can either be up-to-the-minute or woefully out-of-date. Some general Web sites, such as Craigslist or Monster.com, offer up science and environmental positions on occasion. But the following are sites specifically tailored to the latest in green/environmental jobs. Be aware that another problem with anything on the Web is that the site might not be there tomorrow.

- Canadian Environmental Network (CEN) (www.cen-rce .org/eng/index.html). The CEN is a network of environmental NGOs in Canada. Although this is not specifically a job site, this organization comprises the major environmental groups in Canada, and the site is an essential resource for anyone looking for an NGO green collar position.
- CareerEco (www.careereco.com). Billed as "a community where the eco-minded go," CareerEco is a new addition to the field of integrated green job Web sites. The site is divided into the usual jobs/news sections, as well as a blog and a comprehensive Wiki section compiling information on corporations to nonprofits.
- Civil Engineering Central (www.civilengineeringcentral .wordpress.com). Although it is not specifically directed toward green jobs, this site has a constantly updated jobs board, as well as a wide variety of articles and sources for civil engineering professionals.
- CleanTechies (cleantechies.com). This is another full-service site offering jobs, blogs, industry news, a bookstore, and helpful features, such as a résumé tutorial. CleanTechies is also active as a group on LinkedIn.com.

- Eco.org (www.eco.org). This new Web page is modeled after social networking sites. Visitors can join the site and create a profile, join in discussions, upload their résumés, or post jobs. There are blogs and a small news section. The site also boasts an impressive array of international visitors (tallied on a table at the bottom of the screen).
- EcoEmploy (www.ecoemploy.com/jobs/). This is a no-frills board for the latest in general environmental jobs in both the private and public sector, including federal agency jobs. The jobs are mainly in the United States and Canada.
- Ecological Society of America Listserv (listserv.umd.edu/ archives/ecolog-l.html). This offers a weekly listserv—with jobs openings, grant opportunities, calls for papers, seminars, and training events. As an example, the week of July 1, 2009, shows listings for a postdoctoral position in plant-herbivore interactions, a review of a new ecology book, a call for papers for a phrenology conference, and a workshop on statistical analysis for population ecology.
- Environmental Careers Center (www.environmentalcareer.com). Formerly known as the Environmental Careers Center, the group recently changed its name to the Green Careers Center. The site has listing for hundreds of general environmental jobs. The organization also hosts regular seminars and conferences, a green jobs newsletter, and will launch a nationwide environmental professional survey to get a much-needed picture of the job market in the environmental field.
- Environmental Career Opportunities (www.ecojobs.com). The site is a huge repository of environmental jobs: environmental advocacy, international positions, academia, environmental law, education and outreach, and ecotourism jobs.
- Environmental Expert (www.environmental-expert.com). Environmental expert is a Web site with lots of general information and news about a variety of environmental issues. It also has a searchable job board, with positions in the major green categories from the United States and internationally. It's free to sign up, and registered users can post résumés, search jobs, and sign up for job alerts that show when a specific job type comes available.
- Five Million Green Jobs (www.5milliongreenjobs.org/). This site is a resource for green training, green universities, and a place to put your résumé together for a green career.

- Good Work Canada (www.goodworkcanada.ca/). This site was started in 2001 and is one of the older green job sites around. The jobs are located mainly in Canada and feature the usual assortment of clean energy, sustainability, and green marketing jobs. There are also internship and volunteer opportunities available.
- Great Green Careers (www.greatgreencareers.com/). A Web site owned by the publishers of *Mother Jones* and *Utne Reader* magazines, Great Green Careers is a sleek, savvy Web portal that brings together businesses and job hunters. The site offers jobs from full-time to internships, ranging from alternative energy to public sector science positions.
- Green Careers (www.geocities.com/greencareers/). Advertised as the first consulting company to help clients transition into sustainable career paths, the company also offers programs and seminars on green careers.
- Green Collar Blog (www.greencollarblog.org/). On June 23, 2009, the Green Collar Blog's featured job of the day was for an engineer for Solar Design Associates in Massachusetts. After looking through the job description, the site visitor could look through other job boards, research reports on green jobs, find out about upcoming conferences, sign up for the blog's Twitter page, or browse through dozens of topics relating to green jobs.
- Green Collar Vets (www.greencollarvets.org). This is a unique site linking military veterans with green job opportunities and training programs. The jobs generally fall into construction and alternative energy, but other types are also featured. There is a place to donate to the site to help pay for its maintenance.
- Green Dream Jobs (www.sustainablebusiness.com/index.cfm/go/greendreamjobs.main). This site lists jobs across North America—from general nature jobs to outside-the-box green marketing positions—and has areas of the Web site dedicated to networking. A good all-around resource for green job seekers.
- Green Gigs (greengigs.blogspot.com/). Green Gigs is a unique green job Web site that focuses on home-based businesses and telecommuting. What can be greener than not using any fossil fuel to get to work? The blog is updated almost daily with new job openings and tips for working from home.
- Green Jobs Feed (greenjobfeed.com/). A unique job site, with continuous feeds of openings in various green job sectors. The job announcements link to outside sites, such as Monster.com, or to specific green careers job boards.

- Green Jobs Network (www.greenjobs.net/). The Network offers a wide range of general green jobs openings, from clean technologies to alternative energy. It also has a listing of major green job fairs across the country, a green jobs e-mail list, and lists of jobs by states and cities.
- LinkedIn (www.linkedin.com). LinkedIn is a business networking site that is among the most popular on the Web. Designed primarily to make business contacts, it also has a number of groups dedicated to green careers. Job openings are often posted, as are discussions about current trends in green careers and general environmental issues that may affect certain career paths in the future. It's one of the must-join Web sites for serious job seekers and those looking to advance in their field. Job seekers should also not overlook Facebook and Twitter. Many companies in the green collar field have a presence on these sites, and it may be an easy and more efficient way to keep up with job openings and career opportunities.
- Sea Grant Jobs (www.mid-atlantic.seagrant.org/Jobs/). The Sea Grant program is a joint effort between NOAA and academic institutions and other research entities to work on issues relating to the coastline of the United States (despite the name Sea Grant, states such as Ohio have the program). Jobs are primarily in the marine and water research professional vein, but there are other job titles, as well as volunteer and internship opportunities. It's a great resource for anyone looking into a marine science career.
- Sustain Lane (www.sustainlane.com/green-jobs). This is a good, general green job career board with searchable database. Sustain Lane also has a section called "Green Jobs Success Stories," with stories from people on the front lines of the green revolution. It offers real-life examples of what does and doesn't work in the job market.
- Sustainable Industries (www.sustainableindustries.com). A massive site, covering a lot of different green job sectors, this Web site has online videos, Web conferences, active discussion forums, job boards, and news feeds on various sustainable jobs and leading companies in the field.
- Texas Green Jobs (texas.greenjobs.net/). This is just what the name says, a directory of green jobs in Texas, from green building to renewable energy.
- Work Cabin (workcabin.ca). This site is the largest Canadian green jobs board. It has advice articles for employers

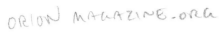
and job-seekers, a regularly updated blog on green career issues specific to Canada, a wide assortment of both green and general scientific positions, and an environmental law section. The site also offers news feeds on alternative energy, conservation, and sustainability.

Associations/Organizations/Conferences

The following are but a small cross-section of the hundreds of national organizations dedicated to environmental and green careers. And new ones are emerging all the time, many at state and local levels. The benefits to joining one of these groups are varied, but all the groups have one thing in common—they allow people to network and socialize, which is one of the single most effective ways not only to get jobs, but to keep on top of developments and trends in the job market.

Also listed are various regional and national conferences. Because green conferences are a relatively new concept, many of these organizations have only been around a short time. Some, such as Opportunity Green, are already becoming known as idea factories of green businesses and careers.

- Green Jobs Conference (www.greenjobsconference.org). The first conference was held in mid-2008. The green jobs conference brings together leaders in the green field from government, NGOs, business, and industry.
- National Association of Environmental Professionals (NAEP) (www.naep.org). The NAEP is a nationwide organization, with 19 state chapters across the country, as well as various smaller subchapters. This organization is a professional association for the advancement of environmental careers that fosters discussion among various science and environmental disciplines; hosts luncheon, workshops, social events, and an annual conference; and promotes job opportunities and career advancement for students and professionals alike.
- National Association for EHS Management (NAEM) (www.naem.org). The NAEM is national organization for environmental leaders in business and industry. The association hosts Web seminars, training courses, conferences, workshops, and career development. By focusing on the private sector, the association offers a unique business-centered perspective. The Web site also has a job board for members.

- Northwest Environmental Business Council (www.nebc.org/). This group's tagline is "the environment is our business." Formed in 1986, this regional council encompasses a wide variety of sustainability and green business as well as more traditional engineering companies.
- Opportunity Green (www.opportunitygreen.com/). This organization holds annual conferences that bring together a disparate yet complimentary cross-section of the latest thinkers, entrepreneurs, visionaries, and business leaders in green companies— established companies that are going green, nonprofits, scientists, and policymakers. The group's main event is an annual conference in November that started in 2007.
- Sustainable Florida-Collins Center (www.sustainableflorida .org). This is the organization for which Tim Center, author of this book's Foreword, is the director. It started as a legislature-created environmental education program, before expanding and breaking off to form its own nonprofit. In 2004, Sustainable Florida merged with the Collins Center for Public Policy. The Center's main goal is to stimulate the use of sustainable business practices in Florida—through outreach, conferences, symposiums, and working with higher education institutions throughout the state to develop sustainability as a cornerstone of environmental education programs.

CHAPTER 3

WATER, WATER, EVERYWHERE

Water is, of course, essential to life. But it is also essential to green jobs. Water is a resource that has a high value, both environmentally and economically. In fact, some political scientists see water supplanting oil as the next natural resource that wars will be fought over. Water resources, both conservation and quality, have been a part of the sciences for years. But water scarcity, drought, increased population growth on the coastlines, declining fish stocks, increasing nutrient loading to water bodies, and an overall trend toward improving water infrastructure have been a boon for professionals in the water field. "About 65 percent of the jobs today are with companies that recycle waste, cut greenhouse gas pollution and handle water conservation,"[1] and the types of jobs that exist in the industry are varied, ranging from "senior project leaders responsible for overseeing large civil engineering works to biological monitoring and water treatment roles within environmental health."[2]

In the area of water supply, careers that include designing systems to collect, filter, and transport high-quality drinking water are in high demand in the United States, but even more so in developing nations, where the local talent and investment to bring potable water to the populace are often not there. In this context, there are NGO and advocacy group options for people looking to get into that line of water-related work. In the United States, the aging and crumbling infrastructure of the water system has been buoyed by investment from the federal government. But professionals in the field question whether there is enough investment to bring the changes and updates to the system that are needed. Nevertheless, the job prospects are looking up. Also needed are water-quality professionals. This line of work dovetails into other green jobs, such as green building and landscape architecture, but also fits in with engineering, chemistry, and biology.

Here is a little background on some pertinent legislation that really drives a lot of the job growth in the industry. The Clean Water Act (CWA) of 1972 was one of the most far-reaching pieces of environmental regulation ever passed by the U.S. Congress. But, although it has been almost 40 years since that landmark legislation, the ramifications of the bill have only recently emerged, as regulations affecting stormwater and water quality have become more stringent and many communities are going to be affected by federal Total Maximum Daily Load rules (TMDL). It wasn't until 1987 that non–point source pollution, primarily caused by stormwater runoff, was addressed under the CWA. National Pollutant Discharge Elimination System (NPDES) permits were established and designed to control runoff by regulating discharges to water bodies.

NPDES permits regulate stormwater discharges from industrial sources as well as municipal separate storm sewer systems (MS4s), which are referred to as Phase I (larger communities) and Phase II (smaller communities) permits. These permits have burdened a lot of underbudgeted and understaffed municipalities. In turn, this has given rise to a need for professionals to assist local and state governments in both an in-house and a consultant capacity to navigate through the permits, assist with compliance, and formulate strategies to help the governments achieve a reduction in non–point source pollution. Similarly, industrial permit holders often need the same type of assistance and more readily outsource to consultants and private businesses to help them in their compliance efforts.

The act of reducing pollution under these regulations was the catalyst for the emergence of a slew of companies who manufacture products designed to assist communities and local governments to meet the sometimes burdensome (and costly) requirements. This is where the fields of science, engineering, and marketing meet. To comply fully with the federal water-quality requirements, companies are expanding their testing of products in laboratories, giving a perfect entry to those looking for a more research-driven job in the water-resources field. These companies are present at trade shows and conferences, places that are always a good idea to attend for potential job seekers or people looking to network in the professional community. It's also a good idea to pay attention to the vendors. Many of them are often looking for new talent to come on board, especially people who have been working in either the regulatory agencies or for local governments. One other thing that you'll find is that the representatives for the vendor companies are usually younger. These companies need high-level, energetic, and driven employees to both design and market the product. Alternately, vendor professionals can also use the conferences as a way to get up to speed on the research and regulatory issues—not only to expand their knowledge base to help them with their jobs, but to have the tools needed to make a move to a public agency or consulting firm.

Most of the products that are featured at water-related conferences are either for utility applications or for dealing with water-quality issues. One of the interesting side fields in water resources is sort of a combination of the two fields and one that has serious future job potential. The niche area is looking at how to utilize the resource to reduce dependency on groundwater for nonpotable uses. Golf courses and some homeowners have systems tied to local stormwater ponds in order to pump the water for irrigation. Rain barrels and cisterns have long been a means for individuals and businesses to use water from downspouts for a variety of purposes. The idea of grey water being used to wash cars and clothes or serve as the water in a toilet bowl makes theoretical sense. There's no need to use valuable potable water for these tasks. But, as a large scale application, the question is still open, and, as with any open question, the possible answers might prove to be the catalyst for a new technology or company to come along with an innovative solution.

Engineers are working with communities to design new and expand existing reclaimed-water systems. Cities in Florida, such as Dunedin and St. Petersburg, have been using reclaimed water for irrigation for quite some time, but the practice is still in its infancy in many parts of the country. The idea of using reclaimed water for irrigation is gaining favor where groundwater resources are suffering. As with the water usage for toilets and car washing, there is no real need to use potable water to water lawns. Reclaimed-water systems are also being used to irrigate golf courses and public parks, and they have a great potential as agricultural irrigation techniques. The only issue with the agricultural application is the cost of the piping to bring the reclaimed water to the farms if those farms are too far outside the municipality's sewer system.

So how does this fit in the green revolution? Water-resource engineering has been around for a while. In fact, water-quality professionals such as Elie Araj have been "preaching environmental conservation for years. Working on the NPDES permits, for example, educating folks to keep fertilizer out of ponds and protecting wetlands from impacts, has been going since the late 1980s early 1990s. We figured out that we have to protect and conserve and when we can enhance and restore."[3] And now the new enthusiasm surrounding environmental stewardship is bringing the effects of stormwater runoff, water-supply safety, and water-supply quantity to the front page of newspapers and into nightly news reports. This is not only an issue in coastal communities, but in any place with economically and ecologically important water resources such as lakes, rivers, ponds, and streams. It goes from the local homeowner's association with a lime green pond in its common area to a community that depends on the quality of a recreationally important lake for tourism dollars. And this new call to action, coupled with the dovetailing increase in regulation, has given the field a renewed sense of purpose.

With that new sense of purpose comes new job opportunities. For all the ups and downs in the environmental industry, water resources is one growth area that seems to be always on the upswing. The growth might not be exponential, but it is steady. From the time I started in the field in 1995 to the present, I've witnessed a huge increase in the number of professionals in the water-resources field, just in Florida. And when you go to national conferences that get bigger every year, it's apparent that water-resource jobs are here to stay and grow.

Another big area of growth in water resources—and another reason that the field has the base to be a sustained growth niche—is the aging and crumbling infrastructure of the water systems throughout the United States. In many older cities, the infrastructure has not been updated in over 100 years and is starting to fall apart. There are estimates for various water professional organizations putting the price tag in the tens of billions of dollars. That's just with the current condition of many of these water-distribution systems, not to mention aging sewer and storm sewer systems. The problem with the issue of water-system infrastructure is that, although it's a necessity from an engineer's point of view, funding from the government often takes a backseat to more pressing infrastructure issues, such as new roads to accommodate poorly planned growth, or pet projects from local representatives. There is only now beginning to be a push to get really serious about addressing water infrastructure. And this is a perfect time for people who are interested in the field, especially in water-resources engineering, to get the training and education they need. The stimulus package passed by Congress in early 2009 dedicated $ 6.4 billion to water and wastewater projects. But professional organizations, such as the Water

Infrastructure Network, have supported funding upward of $20 billion, stating that this kind of investment can create over 700,000 jobs.[4] The Infrastructure Network was unable to get this additional funding in the stimulus package, but the package brought additional awareness about the importance of water infrastructure and how it's a key component to the green jobs career path.

Education and Training

Most water-resources professionals have a degree in engineering. Originally an offshoot of either environmental or civil engineering, water-resources engineering has grown into its own discipline, combining elements of hydrology, engineering, planning, biology, and water quality. Other water-resource professionals have backgrounds in biology or chemistry. Both of these naturally fall in with water-quality work and effectiveness of stormwater and wastewater projects. The number of universities and colleges offering degrees in the field has expanded in recent years.

You can also work your way up into water-resource positions. Your local Public Works Department is a great place to start. Beginning with a field crew can give you the real in-the-field experience that can help as you move up the ladder. This way is better if you plan on staying in a municipal position. A lot of municipalities also pay for continuing training to keep job skills current. This is especially helpful in the wastewater field. Most private consulting and engineering firms require at least a bachelor's degree, with years of experience, to move further up the job chain.

There are many schools with top-quality engineering programs, both civil and environmental. With the focus on water-resource regulations increasing, schools are seeing a shift in their engineering departments, reflecting the new importance of stormwater runoff control, water supply, water-quality monitoring, and wastewater systems. Another area that a potential water-resource professional should become fluent in is computer water modeling. Modeling is a specialized part of the larger water-resources job niche, but it is increasingly important to understanding the dynamics of water, in both storm events and circulation models. Most schools with water-resources degree programs offer courses in computer modeling programs and GIS. It's advisable to take at least one of these courses.

The following schools and training centers represent a small sample of what's out there. Take the time to research the school that best fits your needs before deciding where to go. Many schools now offer online classes for people looking to get back into school after an absence and for those wanting to go for advanced degrees yet still have to work 40 hours per week.

- Certified Professional in Erosion and Sediment Control™ (www.cpesc.org). This is national certification that's recognized across the construction, development, and environmental professions. The company also offers erosion and sediment control inspector certification, as well as professional water-quality certification. The trainings are often held in conjunction with national stormwater conferences.
- New Jersey Water Resources Research Institute (njwrri.rutgers .edu). Affiliated with Rutgers College, the Institute brings together professional and academics from across the state to "train students at the undergraduate, graduate and postgraduate levels to become the next generation of water resource professionals for New Jersey."
- Online Wastewater training (www.onlinewastewatertraining .com/). The site offers various wastewater training programs, customized for specific state requirements.
- Onsite Wastewater Training Centers. There are various training centers that offer onsite programs for professionals in the onsite wastewater field. Training centers are located in Iowa, Kentucky, Utah, Alabama, Rhode Island, and Virginia.
- Oregon State University/Water Resources Program (oregonstate .edu/gradwater/). This program offers master's and Ph.D. degrees in water resources, with specializations in water-resources engineering, water-resources science, and water-resources policy and management.
- Stevens Institute of Technology (New York City). Stevens offers an engineering master's degree with a concentration in water resources. The degree concentrates on non–point source pollutions, water quality, wetland issues, and general water engineering. A graduate certificate (completion of four courses) is also offered.
- Stormwater USA (www.stormwaterusa.com). This private company offers specialized stormwater training and certifications, including a Certified Compliance Inspector of Stormwater, Certified Preparer of SWPPP (stormwater pollution prevention plans), and Home Depot stormwater training, a mandatory course for some employees of the retail giant.

- University of Central Florida/Stormwater Management Academy (www.stormwater.ucf.edu/). This center, affiliated with the university, is one of the premier stormwater education and research facilities in the country. Professionals work on a variety of research projects regarding Best Management Practices (BMPs) stormwater runoff control, and public education and outreach, and they host conferences, trainings, and seminars for professional development. The college itself offers a master's degree program in water resources.
- University of Florida/Master of Science (online) (www .distancelearning.ufl.edu/program.aspx?p=60). This 30-hour online master's course is for a Master of Science or Engineering degree in Environmental Engineering Sciences: Water, Wastewater, and Stormwater Engineering. This unique online opportunity mixes traditional engineering design with biology, water policy, and planning. The university campus also houses the Water Resources Research Center. The Center works on water-resource projects with other institutions of higher learning, as well as with public agencies in Florida. There is also technology-specific research being done at the Center.
- University of Minnesota (wrs.umn.edu). The University's Water Resources Science Department offers graduate degrees in water resources, with concentrations in a variety of areas, including hydrology, limnology, and watershed management. Master's as well as Ph.D. degrees are available.
- University of New Hampshire/UNH Stormwater Center (www.unh.edu/erg/cstev/). The Stormwater Center tests stormwater management technologies and serves as a technical resource for stormwater professionals. The Center also offers workshops, such as a recent one on permeable pavement.
- University of North Carolina's Stormwater Engineering Team (www.bae.ncsu.edu/stormwater/team.htm). The Team is a group "consisting of tenure and non–tenure track faculty, graduate students, part-time associates, and off-campus Extension Faculty." They work on stormwater research topics, such as BMP design and efficiency, maintenance of stormwater systems, economic impact of stormwater treatment, and bioretention areas. The Center offers offsite outreach programs, including the Home*A*Syst education program to teach homeowners about residential stormwater management, planting and designing backyard rain gardens,

and providing NPDES Phase II permit education requirements for local communities.

Places to Work

The Public Sector: With the way the economy ebbs and flows, sometimes job security can mean more than pay or benefits. Although most
government jobs can provide both in a reasonable range, many entry-
level positions are on the lower end of the scale and may not have benefits, particularly field jobs. However, if you are looking to go into
stormwater engineering or water-quality related work, your local public
works, utilities, or environmental services department may be just the
right choice.

Public works or specific stormwater departments are responsible for
most of the major construction in towns, cities, and counties. They usually
employ engineers from entry level up to seasoned professionals. It's also a
place where you can get a lot of on-the-job training. Public agencies are
usually amenable to sending their employees to training, as well as providing tuition reimbursement for those wanting to go back to school.
Many government agencies have a depth of experience that young private
firms lack. The engineering field is a graying one, and it's more important
than ever not only to attract top young talent to the field but to pass on the
knowledge that a couple decades of experience bring to the table.

Utilities departments are less likely to need straight stormwater work
but often need those who can blend knowledge of water quality and
water-resources management. These departments are always looking for
innovative thinkers to look at the usual problems of water supply and
demand in new ways. As previously mentioned, reuse of stormwater is a
growing field of inquiry and will be a natural supplement to water supplies operated by utilities departments.

The pros of working in the public sector include job security. There's
a reason many people stay in government positions for a long time. It's
rewarding work with good pay, but the fact that jobs are rarely shed and
the retirement benefits are usually high make it an attractive place to
work throughout your career. One of the biggest cons relates to that job
security. With so many long-term employees taking the higher-level
positions, it's often difficult to advance upward. Rigidity in organiza-
tional charts keeps lower-level employees at their positions for longer
than in the private sector.

Consulting Firms: For some in the public sector, a move to the private
marketplace is a logical next step to advance their careers. The perfect

marriage of science and commerce is consulting firms. Most are anchored by engineering, but others are primarily environmental firms, focusing on biology-driven projects. Throughout this guide, various consulting firms are profiled, many filling a wide variety of general environmental and green jobs; other serve a specific niche market.

The primary jobs of firms that work in water-resource-related fields are to assist government agencies in planning, designing, and permitting of their stormwater drainage systems. Other services include NPDES permitting, TMDL assistance, project consultation, and water-quality monitoring. Because many of the governments face budget shortfalls, they are forced to outsource services relating to water quality. Though not often thought of as essential services, the NPDES and TMDL programs are federally mandated, which means that, like it or not, the local and state governments need to comply.

One of the best ways to look at environmental consulting firms is to attend a conference or join a local association of stormwater professionals. Networking is the best way to know who is doing what, who is hiring, and what you'll need to be a competitive candidate should any job opening emerge. For those just starting out in the field, many firms offer paid internships and entry-level scientist positions as a way to get your feet wet.

Unlike the public sector, private firms are profit-driven, so when work is slow, there is always a danger of being laid off. Employees can sometimes work long hours if projects are due or spend more time in the field than their public sector counterparts. The flip side is that consulting firms offer generally higher wages and, because of the often fluid nature of the business, more opportunities for advancement.

Manufacturers/Emerging Technologies Companies

For innovative thinkers, for engineers looking to work at the edge of innovation, for scientists with a flair for sales, or for businesspeople and entrepreneurs simply looking to expand into a nontraditional area, emerging technologies in water quality and stormwater-runoff prevention are an expanding market. These technologies are developed by mainly smaller companies, operating without major corporate backing. When you get into utility work and large-scale pumps, you'll get the big companies, such as Siemens, in the mix, but in water-quality niche markets, it's strictly the smaller guys. And that opens up the door for potential job opportunities and ideas for water-resource entrepreneurs looking to start their own water-technology company.

There are literally hundreds of devices to deal with water-quality issues and flooding problems. If you add in products that are designed for sediment and erosion control, the number jumps up dramatically. As an example, two common types of water-quality control devices are baffle boxes and continuous deflection systems (CDS units). Baffle boxes and CDS units are designed to be placed in storm drain inlets. They capture floating particles and debris, filter out hydrocarbons, oil, and grease; and, as a result, they remove Total Suspended Solids (TSS) and nutrients from the outflow. These units are often expensive, but in built-out urban areas, they offer one of the few ways to meet water-quality goals. Places without open land for stormwater treatment ponds often have few options. But the units are big sellers. Municipalities that are built-out and dense urban centers use these products to deal with stormwater runoff. As an employee of the company, you would help customers decide the best option for their needs, work with the engineer to get the product specs correct, and ensure that the installation goes smoothly and that any maintenance problems are handled without issues.

One thing to note is that a lot of these companies are not only based in the United States but do their manufacturing here as well. Growth in this area could help, albeit slightly, to offset the increasing shedding of manufacturing jobs overseas, as well as those lost to increased productivity. Although most of these companies are small, they require people with high-tech proclivity. Even the manufacturing staff includes people with enough specialized training to do the job. As in the case of many of the manufacturing jobs in this book, for these jobs, we are mostly past the days when a person can walk off the street and go to work in a factory. To stay competitive in the job market, as well as compete in an uneven and unfair global manufacturing field, innovation and flexibility are two key factors.

Here are a few of the companies working in the field.

- Contech (www.contech-cpi.com). Contech specializes in stormwater and stabilization technologies and products. Contech is one of the larger companies in the field.
- Sun Tree Technologies (www.suntreetech.com). Sun Tree designs and manufacturers baffle boxes and other stormwater treatment systems.
- Bay Saver (www.baysaver.com/). Bay Save is another leading company in stormwater treatment technology.
- North American Green (www.nagreen.com/). North American Green is the world's leading manufacturer of sediment and erosion control products.

Networking Resources

- The American Public Works Association (APWA) (www.apwa
  .net). The APWA is mainly an organization for municipal public
  works professionals, although many consulting companies and
  private firms belong as well. Their annual conference is a must-
  attend for professionals in general wastewater and water-supply
  positions. It offers a variety of seminars and workshops, as well
  as training sessions, networking opportunities, and exhibitors.
  The APWA also has a young professionals group and various
  Web-based seminars and trainings, and it holds local chapter
  seminars across the country.
- American Society of Civil Engineers (ASCE) (www.asce.org).
  The ASCE is an organization that holds conferences, trainings,
  workshops, and symposiums. Founded in 1852, it's one of the
  most respected professional organizations in the world. It has
  over 140,000 members worldwide and is active in a wide variety
  of policy issues relating to engineering. The organization has a
  number of technical committees, publishes studies in 31 journals, and is involved in a myriad of projects. For the job seeker,
  the ASCE offers a wealth of education and training opportunities, including conferences. Local ASCE chapters also hold educational luncheons, which serve a dual purpose of career
  development and networking.
- American Water Works Association (AWWA) (www.awwa.org).
  It's the oldest water-related professional organization around,
  founded in 1881. The AWWA has over 60,000 members and is
  a leader in advocacy and education related to safe public drinking water and other water-resource-related issues. The AWWA
  is involved with water policy and education and outreach, and it
  holds annual conferences and offers numerous training opportunities for its members.
- Global Water Partnership (www.gwpforum.org). This worldwide organization, founded by the World Bank, is tasked with
  promoting sustainable development as it relates to the protection
  of water resources. The Partnership's main focus is on drinking
  water supply and safety issues. The group is active in 70 countries. There are also smaller regional organizations, especially in
  Third World countries, that deal with water-supply issues.
- National Water Resources Association (www.nwra.org). This
  group comprises primarily Western state water-resource agencies,
  private companies, and water districts. The mission is to protect

and properly manage water resources. The Association's Web site says the group was formally established in 1932 and is active in working with congressional representatives on water-use issues.

- Stormcon® (www.stormcon.com). Stormcon is the world's largest stormwater conference, with hundreds of exhibitors and thousands of attendees. The conferences usually alternate between the East Coast, Midwest, South, and West Coast of the United States. In addition to the various conference proceedings, exhibit halls, and talks, there are workshops and trainings for certifications and continuing credits for professionals who need to stay current in their respective fields.

- WEFTEC (www.weftec.org). The Water Environment Federation's annual conference, with professionals from the stormwater field as well as wastewater and water quality, is one of the largest water-based conferences in the country, with thousands of exhibitors and ten times more attendees. The conference is usually a week-long affair, with the usual mix of networking opportunities and trainings interspersed with the poster sessions and talks. WEFTEC also has an active young engineer group, which is a great networking option for students just entering the job market.

- IECA (www.ieca.org). The International Erosion Control Association is a professional organization for professionals in sediment and erosion control. A majority of the more than 3,000 members are in the construction or public works industry; many others are involved in stormwater-related fields. The IECA hosts a large annual conference. Like many conferences, it's a worthwhile mix of education and fun.

Employment Outlook

State and federal water-quality requirements are not going away. In many cases, they are getting stricter. In states like Florida, the TMDL process is still in its beginning stages, and communities, strapped for cash, will be looking at innovative and cost-effective methods of complying with the new standards. Stormwater management has, for many years, been dominated by the conveyance mentality—get it off the road and into the nearest receiving water body as quick as possible. It's only recently that the water-quality aspect has become the focal point.

Water-supply matters, especially in some foreign countries, are always going to be an issue, especially with a rapidly expanding population. The need for qualified water professionals is growing rapidly.

Because there is a need to comply with these rules, local and state governments, despite budget cutbacks, are going to need people to take charge of keeping their permits in compliance, design stormwater systems that encourage water-quality improvements as well as provide maximum drainage, review proposals for new developments, develop strategies to retrofit existing developments, and, of course, deal with politicians. Even though this is often the job of a public employee, there will be a need for consultants.

Consulting firms can capitalize on the shrinking budgets by helping governments streamline their operation, come up with innovative designs, bring in expertise that the government agencies might not have, and keep a tight work schedule based on an agreed-upon contract. Consultants also play a vital role in emerging technology companies by assisting with development and with efficiency studies and, as a marketing force, recommending certain products to their clients.

Another reason that this field will be growing in the near future is demographics. Engineering is increasingly an aging field, with fewer graduates coming down the pike. Says one pundit, "The perception of the engineer has fallen to that of a grumpy, middle-aged, mustachioed man awaiting retirement by quoting Monty Python."[5] There has been a push on—from public schools implementing a STEM (Science, Technology, Engineering, and Math) approach to a renewed concentration at universities—to expand environmental curriculums to attract new students.

This issue is not limited to the United States. The Confederation of British Industry warned that "a growing crisis threatens to engulf British businesses because of the slump in the number of manufacturing and engineering graduates coming out of UK universities."[6]

Whatever the choice, the stormwater, wastewater, and hydrology industry is a growing one, and it's an industry that is at the leading edge of the green movement, addressing regulatory, biological, physical, and economical concerns. The job market has been expanding at a steady clip, and it shows no signs of abating. For those interested in a dynamic field with elements of engineering, biology, and environmental science, stormwater and water quality may be the right fit.

Job Resources

The following is a list of some major organizations, job sites, and references to assist you in finding positions in the water-resources field. In addition to the following sites, you can also find job openings on general career sites, some university Web pages, and on other environmental career job boards. For positions in local and state government agencies, it's best to visit those specific sites. They often have more up-to-date position descriptions and don't always list on major career Web sites.

- Engineering-Jobs Site (www.engineering-job-site.com/). A general job board for all types of engineering positions across the country, this site has water-resource positions listed, and the database is searchable by specialty.
- Graduating Engineer (www.graduatingengineer.com/resources/future-of-your-field). Graduating Engineer is a repository of resources for the graduating engineer, from the latest news to jobs. The site has a section with a comprehensive search engine for college and graduate schools that specialize in engineering, as well as practical articles on subjects such as job interviews and networking.
- Hydrogeology, Hydrology, and Water Resources Jobs (www.earthworks-jobs.com/hydro.htm). This is a no-frills site for water-resource jobs in the United States, Canada, and Europe. The greater Earth Work site is an excellent source not only for green jobs but for general science positions, both national and international.
- Hydro Web (hydroweb.com/). This is the home Web site of the International Association of Environmental Hydrology. The group produces a peer-reviewed journal, which is available online. The site also has discussion groups, general news in hydrology, and career resources.
- Spatial Hydrology Jobs (www.spatialhydrology.com/joblinks .html). An interesting resource for professionals in GIS, hydrology, and modeling, to look for available positions in the three fields. As GIS and computer modeling become increasingly important to the water-resource field, these segments will lead to jobs more and more.
- Stormwater Authority (www.stormwaterauthority.org/). This site is a great one-stop shop for stormwater news and events; it is split into separate sections for engineers, site developers, and contractors and is one of the most comprehensive stormwater sites online.
- *Stormwater* magazine (www.stormh20.com/). *Stormwater* magazine is the premier journal for everything related to stormwater. This site is a companion to the print version, but with added features, such as a message board and news feeds. Besides serving

as a great networking opportunity, the message boards can have leads for vacant positions.

- Stormwater Manager's Resource Center (www.stormwatercenter .net/). This is a no-frills site with research papers on a variety of stormwater topics. Although not technically a job site, it's a good stop for background research on topics in water quality.
- Stormwater Jobs (www.stormwaterjobs.com/). As the name says, this Web site is a resource for jobs in the stormwater, surface water, hydrology, and wastewater engineering fields. It's one of the most comprehensive in the water-resources field.
- United States Geological Survey (USGS) (www.usgs.gov). The USGS science programs span geology, geography, biology, and a particular emphasis on water resources. The USGS is involved with a lot of monitoring of lakes, rivers, and streams and often works on projects in estuarine and marine environments. Job opportunities include everything from entry-level to advanced-degree positions.
- Water Environment Federation Job Site (www.wef.org/ MembershipCareers/JobBank/). The Water Environment Federation, who put on the annual WEFTEC shows, have a good job board of members of the organization. They also have a young engineer program that helps recent graduates with networking, career opportunities, and professional development. The jobs are in all fields of water resources, from quality to quantity.
- Water and Wastewater Jobs (www.waterandwastewaterjobs .com/). An industry-based Web site, this site has a place to post résumés, search for jobs, look through employer profiles, and catch up on the latest news in water resources. It alternates between hard engineering and more green-oriented jobs.

CHAPTER 4

IMAGINING NEW POWER

When people think of green jobs, the one sector that most commonly comes to mind is alternative and renewable energy. Oil prices have gone through wild fluctuations through the latter half of the 2000s, and geopolitical fallout from the Iraq war has led to calls for a lessening of dependence on foreign oil. Environmental activists are looking for ways to wean the country from its coal-driven power plants, citing a variety of environmental issues—including the acceleration of global climate change and air pollution. The panacea for these issues seems to be alternative and renewable energy. The big five are wind, solar, geothermal, biofuels, and nuclear.[1]

The change to a more renewable-energy driven economy has been pushed forward by environmental activists, the science community, and world government. Starting with the Kyoto protocol through the most recent legislation, the American Clean Energy and Security Act regarding carbon emission in the United States, there is a drive to reduce the global CO_2 emissions in order to curb global climate change. And although there is still some question over the rate of change and the exact adverse effects, there is a palpable sense that change must be made.

Scientists from every field of inquiry have made similar observations about the rate of change and the issues that the whole world will face if action is not taken to reduce emissions. There are some who think that global climate change can be explained by natural processes, pointing to rapid shift in climate throughout Earth's history. Others point to the unprecedented pace of change since the start of the Industrial Revolution. Although the exact cause is unknown, there is more certainty that the climate is undergoing a change, and the evidence points to anthropogenic causes.

One method that traditional oil energy producers are looking at to reduce CO_2 and greenhouse gas emissions is a process called carbon capture and sequestration (CCS) technology. The concept is simple in theory. Carbon dioxide is captured during the refining process and compressed into a liquid form. The liquid is then injected deep underground to store and sequester. These underground carbon storage units reabsorb the carbon into the substrate or ocean environment and back into normal physical and biological processes. The first power plant in the United States to use this storage method was in North Dakota, where the carbon was injected into deep wells.

Some of the methods for CCS are aimed at water bodies. The idea of iron fertilization of the oceans is to induce the production of phytoplankton, which in turn absorb greater amounts of CO_2 from the atmosphere as part of their normal daily biological function. This method shows promise, but it's unclear how the addition of iron might affect the chemical balance of the oceans. A similar method using the addition of nitrogen to jump-start additional primary production in the ocean has the potential to reduce greenhouse gasses and also, like the iron fertilization, result in a higher biomass of bottom level food for mid and apex predators. With fish stocks in as dire shape as they are now, the idea that there is a way to increase fish populations—that is, a method in addition to regulations and aquaculture—sounds promising, but there are still the unknowns of the effect on the ocean.

The easiest way to reduce carbon emissions and encourage the increased absorption of CO_2 is to plant trees. Reforestation is an idea that took hold in parts of the world where deforestation is rampant. Coupled with advances in agricultural production, this method can reduce greenhouse gasses to some extent, but it's unclear whether it is enough to have a global effect.

The climate change scenario notwithstanding, the simple fact is that oil, natural gas, and coal are finite resources, albeit with many more years of supply to meet our current energy needs. But our current energy needs have changed dramatically over the last decade. The growth of India and China alone has caused a surge in demand for petroleum-based energy products. Imagine what will happen when Africa rises to the same economic level as China currently is at and China exceeds where the United States is. The thought behind that is not welcoming. Oil prices will undoubtedly rise. The one saving grace in that scenario is that, although China and India are behind other developed nations in embracing alternative forms of energy and working on energy efficiency, they have made enough progress over recent years to cause forecasters to revise downward their predictions for the oil demand coming out of those countries. However, even if they get more efficient, there will still be other emerging economies that will be looking to get a bigger share of the oil pie. That's where sustainable, renewable alternative energy comes into the picture.

There are other ways to expand the production and use of oil-based energy products. Natural gas is an option that is a growing sector of the petroleum-based energy industry. Advances in hydraulic fracturing to break apart rocks to draw to natural gas, horizontal drilling to access hard-to-reach pockets of gas, methane-based natural gas source exploration and extraction, and the extraction of natural gas from the shale formations of the United States and Canada are driving the growth in the natural gas industry. These "unconventional plays from shales, coal bed methane and other sources will account for 53 percent of U.S. and Canadian natural gas supplies within 11 years—up from 30 percent in 2000."[2] But although natural gas has some strengths over coal for powering electrical plants, its use doesn't solve the oil dependency issue from a geopolitical standpoint, even though more of it is domestic compared with straight oil, and certainly it does not fully address emissions issues, although it burns cleaner than other petroleum products.

Coal is one of the dominant natural resources used in electrical power plants for power generation. In the United States, coal accounts for over half the electricity produced, and in some developing countries, such as China, the percentage is closer to 80. All those plants belching smoke into the air are not only a cause for alarm from the climate change science perspective but also from the point of view of general air-quality concerns. In the months running up to the 2008 Summer Olympics in Beijing, Chinese authorities restricted the number of cars on the road and idled some plants to combat the thick coal smog that enveloped the city. Athletes were concerned about the high particulate counts in the air and the potential health ramifications. Asthma has increased in Southeast Asia, by some accounts by over 20 percent. This is seen as a direct result of the rapid urbanization of the region and the relatively dirty power plants.

In the United States, the coal industry has been pushing for clean coal technology. Advocates say that, although it's not the cleanest energy source around, new technologies can significantly reduce the emissions from coal-fueled power plants—not only to be in line with current reg-ulations but to go below them in some cases. Opponents argue that clean coal is a misnomer and that the emissions from coal plants will still affect greenhouse gas production, ultimately driving climate change.

Clean coal technology includes a number of advanced methods to reduce CO_2 and sulfide emissions from the plant stacks. Clean coal is also trying to use CCS technology to reduce CO_2 emissions. Power plants use a variety of methods, from scrubbers to advanced detection equipment, to reduce emission levels. Critics say that even these methods are still allowing large amounts of greenhouse gases in to the atmosphere and that the only way for coal to be truly clean is not to burn it at all. At this time, that is not a practical solution.

Coal also faces criticism from the way in which it's mined. There are areas in West Virginia and Kentucky where mountain tops have been removed to look for coal deposits. This mountain top removal method has come under harsh criticism, not just from environmental groups, who say the destruction to the habitat is dangerous, but from local citizens, who say that the method of mining is dangerous and causes all types of ecological damage to their neighborhoods and homes, as well as damage to rivers and creeks, in the form of high turbidity, localized fish kills, and decreased biodiversity in the water bodies. The flip side, of course, is that the coal industry employs a lot of people in these towns off the beaten path, where there aren't as many job opportunities as in other areas. And in coal country, the geography of the area does not make it conducive to most forms of alternative energy.

Right now it's a public relations battle, but clean coal will probably become the norm for the coal industry. Coal is too important to current power-generation facilities, and to change suddenly the way in which those plants produce electricity would be cost-prohibitive. The next course is to make newer plants look at ways of incorporating alternative energy sources into the coal and natural gas mix. The weaning from a coal-based system can occur more easily this way. It would also mitigate the price differential. By bringing in more expensive renewable energy and mixing it with low-cost coal, the price spike would be a lot more moderate and not cause sticker shock to unsuspecting consumers. This is a way to make a change to alternative energy that is more economically palpable to the general public, apart from people who are environmen-tally conscious and would pay the extra cost no matter what, simply on principle.

The push to wean America from its oil addiction has found propo-nents and opponents in the corridors of governmental power, from state legislatures to the U.S. Congress. But there has been an overall trend in looking toward the future and enacting regulations to curb greenhouse gas emissions in order to reduce potential effects on climate change. With this regulation-driven agenda, the opportunities for real career growth in the areas of the green economy that favor these positions will continue to accelerate, possibly even one day passing the 1.6 million Americans who work in the traditional energy industry.

The move to green energy got some political pull after 9/11, and the push at that time was mainly geopolitical. Taking money out of the hands of some regimes that were hostile to the United States was seen as a patriotic and practical move to ensure the country's safety and to position it to withstand the fluctuations in prices of oil on the world market. That idea was further refined to encompass a more ecologically minded approach. Also among these calls for a move for energy independence was the reality of global climate change and pressure from other countries for the United States to step up to the plate and do its part to reduce emissions and to increase energy efficiency. In mid-2009, the House of Representatives passed the American Clean Energy and Security Act. The Act outlined the bold steps that would be taken to reduce the nation's carbon output by 2020—through both a cap-and-trade program (explained in Chapter 8, Green Law) as well as mandating that power companies generate or purchase 15 percent of their energy from renewable sources. Nuclear was not listed as one of the potential sources, but also missing was hydropower, a type of renewable, zero-emission energy that is common north of the U.S. border. "This predominant source of electricity in Canada is a proven, nonpolluting renewable and effective source of electricity. It's even recognized by environmentalists as a sustainable energy solution."[3]

Regardless of how the country is going to get there, whether by a solar-driven alternative sector or one more dependent on wind power, most green professionals, like Ian Thompson, see a world where various forms of energy will co-exist: "coal will always have an application, solar will have its say with selling, developing, installing, etc."[4] Others envision a world that runs solely on what are now referred to as alternative energies but that one day may become reality. While this change is taking place, it's important to look critically at alternative energies and really assess where they will fit into the national picture and how the various careers in these sectors will evolve.

It should also be noted that some traditional oil companies are already getting into alternative energies. It stands to reason that their motivating factor is primarily the responsibility to turn a profit for their shareholders.

And although a contentious issue at first, it's now apparent that the move by some oil companies into alternative energy production is a shrewd and prescient business move, one designed to keep pace with potential competitors but also to have a fall-back plan for the day when oil runs out. Exxon Mobil has so far stayed out of a lot of alternative energy investment, investing little of its profit into alternative technologies. For such a big company, alternative energy at this time does not make much business sense, and its shareholders have so far resisted any move by board members to bring a more sustainable ethos into the company. Exxon is churning out record profits, so the need to diversify is not that strong. Some say that Exxon will lag behind its competitors and be at a disadvantage when renewables gain a greater share of the market. But, for now, the oil company is raking in the profits. Other oil companies have made the move. British Petroleum (BP) has adopted the moniker "Beyond Petroleum." BP projects are spread across the alternative energy spectrum. They are investors in the largest solar energy installation in Germany, providing solar power to commercial customers, expanding hydrogen power research and development, and working toward adding cleaner burning natural gas facilities into the BP energy portfolio. In fact, BP has made such a major investment in renewables that it's leading the pack among the oil companies. It was a gamble when the company got into the concept, but now it is seeing rewards in profit, cost savings, and in brand recognition.

With even oil companies jumping on the renewable energy bandwagon, it seems that the future is written in stone. The renewable activists and proponents are convinced that a fully alternative-energy driven future is as certain as the setting sun. But first there needs to be a reality check—as to where we currently stand with renewable technology and the real progress we have made. First, alternative energy is bound by many factors, especially cost. Currently, electricity produced by coal is fairly cheap, whereas electricity from alternative sources is more expensive. With economic uncertainty, consumers, more often than not, go to lower prices and an energy source that is readily accessible. Alternative-energy fill-up stations are not easily found, if at all. There is also the real possibility that if a power company decides to supplant its coal-powered plant with, say, wind turbine-generated energy, it will, at least in the short term, raise energy prices. There is the reality that an increase in energy prices will affect less affluent populations. But potential increase in the price of oil-based energy is, of course, equally as plausible. And many opponents of coal point to the environmental costs associated with the oft-maligned source of energy.

Alternative energy cannot be stored as easily as oil and coal can. It's easy to say that wind and sun are always a part of the weather, but it's not true. In Florida, which seems like a natural place to have solar energy be a cornerstone of the state's energy policy, it may be sunny for much of the year, but it also rains quite a bit. The same goes for wind farms in the Great Plains. The wind is seemingly always there, but the velocity varies greatly, affecting the amount of energy produced. There is currently no effective way to store the energy provided by these alternative systems. According to lawyer and author Richard Chapo, "Storage is a huge issue because using alternative energy puts us at the whim of Mother Nature."[5] Geothermal energy for heating and cooling homes and businesses is somewhat more predictable and can probably be a major component of the country's energy strategy over the next decade. And the more so-called far-out scenarios, such as using offshore wave and current energy, are not developed enough yet in this country to be a factor.

BP's Tony Hayward summed up some of the realities of oil and gas:

It is not true to say that we are running out of hydrocarbons. There are nearly 42 years of proved oil reserves left in the ground and 60 years of natural gas. The world has so far produced 1 trillion barrels of oil. We have reserves of a further trillion barrels, and we know where there are another trillion barrels that we have yet to approve. On top of all of that, there are vast quantities of unconventional hydrocarbons, including oil sands, heavy oil and unconventional gas. And there are major hydrocarbon basins such as the Arctic which have yet to be explored.[6]

There is also an argument against alternative energy or, more accurately, a sort of yield sign, to slow things down and look at green energy critically before jumping off the cliff to have everything run on the sun. The easiest way to reduce our dependence on foreign oil is to drill for more in the United States. Or so the argument goes, from polemical statements from those who are not fans of turning all of our energy needs over to renewable means. The truth is that the country is nowhere near being able to do that anyway. The infrastructure of the society is not set up for wind-powered electricity or hydrogen fuel-cell cars. At least not yet. To get up to where these alternative forms of energy will be at least half of the U.S. power supply will likely take decades.

So the notion of a nation operating solely on alternative energy is anything but certain. There is a growing segment of consumers who are looking to use alternative energy. Professionals in the field, such as landscape architect Pat Millington, believe that "any opportunity to save money and preserve the environment will be on the forefront."[7] And although the increased cost at the onset of many of these sources of energy will turn off a majority of people, some see the long-term savings, especially at the residential level, as being a way to make the best choice, from an environmental and economic perspective.

However, a major rise in the availability of alternative energy and a move toward making it a greater proportion of the total energy picture presents some labor challenges. With any new type of career path, there is always the need for trained workers, and currently there is certainly a dearth of people with the necessary skills and training for jobs in the renewable energy fields. "Solar and wind turbine manufacturing plants will need assembly line workers. Mechanics, electricians and mainte-nance workers will be needed for wind farms, solar parks and biofuels plants. And many types of science and engineering positions will be central to the growth of the industry."[8]

Government drives green energy by tax incentives, regulations, and outright spending. Some states, such as Washington, offer tax rebates on energy-efficient appliances and the addition of alternative energy devices to a residence or business.[9] But it's going to be the private sector and the marketplace that will help alternative energy gain a bigger slice of the energy pie, not only in the United States but worldwide. This is espe-cially true in developing countries such as China and India, where economic explosions have caused a rise in environmental issues, driven mainly by power generation using older technologies. And even though large corporations like BP have a leading role in the green energy mar-ketplace, as one expert, Fritz Kreiss, pointed out, "entrepreneurs create the markets on the leading edge. They are the risk takers and once it becomes partly established, then other companies come in to maximize the potential."[10]

What Types of Jobs?

The world of alternative energy offers a wide range of career opportunities—including project management of solar, wind, and geot-hermal installations, plumbers (geothermal), solar cell developers, engi-neers, scientists, construction, energy consultants, manufacturers of alternative energy products, sales, professional services, marketing, and dozens more. Says John Merlino, "These green projects would drive a whole economy inclusive of a few million jobs."[11] A recent study by the University of Massachusetts tallied the green-job impact, with ancillary job sectors, at over 14 million, and suggested that it can expand even more with the promotion of clean energy programs and more job training. In the following sections, we look at jobs and career outlooks for some of the major alternative energy sectors: geothermal, wind, and solar. But not all alternative energy is divvied up into those categories. There are a number of new and emerging technologies that will challenge scientists and entrepreneurs and open up even more opportunities for creative job seekers.

Professionals who are already employed by fossil fuel companies are working at a time when profits are high and jobs are fairly secure, so, at least in the short term, there won't be a transfer of expertise over from one sector to another. Many of the jobs currently in these sectors range from oil workers and drillers to geologists and engineers. These career paths can transfer easily to alternative energy, especially the engineers and field workers. Geologists will be in demand as geothermal energy gains in popularity. But the fact is that the openings are happening now, and the demand for trained professionals is high; as you read this, the current situation offers up a wealth of opportunities for people looking to make their move into the field.

The range of positions available in alternative energy production, manufacturing of materials, and distribution is far-reaching. On the professional side, the following positions are in demand: environmental engineers, electrical and mechanical engineers, chemical engineers, chemists, technicians, and computer programmers. On the more trade-related side, the following positions are in demand: metal workers, iron workers, wind turbine manufacturers, wind turbine mechanics, solar panel installers, metal fabricators, welders, construction and project managers, chemical equipment technicians, and an assortment of jobs relating to the delivery of the energy, not to mention ancillary jobs such as those of truck drivers for the materials and marketers to promote the various companies engaged in alternative energy research and production.

Fuel-cell technology is another growing field. A Texas Renewable Energy Education Consortium chairman told CNN that "100 percent of his graduates find jobs in the fuel-cell industry—many before graduation."[12] Fuel-cell positions are often more research-oriented, and many students with majors in the engineering fields can find work in fuel-cell technology research laboratories. Fuel-cell entrepreneurs are starting up research and technology companies; it is another hot job that is related to alternative energy. In fact, with fuel cells, many highly skilled auto workers who were affected by the auto woes will be able to use their engineering know-how and some work already done by the auto companies on fuel-cell technology and potentially spread that knowledge base around to dozens of small companies, giving the competitive boost that the sector needs. With the competition comes a corresponding rise in the effectiveness of the fuel cells.

Geothermal Energy

Geothermal energy is simply energy from the Earth. It's using the Earth's natural temperature and subterranean heating system to produce power and heat and cool homes. It's gaining acceptance in the United States as a viable alternative energy. In some parts of the world, Iceland for one, geothermal energy has been a staple source of power and heat for many years. The system used to distribute this energy through residential and commercial buildings is relatively simple in that it takes the heat directly from the ground and distributes it throughout the dwelling; the process is reversed for cooling. Another advantage is hot water that doesn't need a hot water heater to store up. Geothermal systems can reduce electricity usage by up to 50 percent from conventional heating and cooling systems. Geothermal heat is also used to provide raw energy to power plants. It's far cleaner than coal and without the side effects of nuclear.

Although some countries, like Iceland, have long enjoyed the benefits of geothermal power, energy from underground has not been as popular in the United States. As of 2008, there were only eight states that were regularly producing geothermal energy: Alaska, California, Hawaii, Idaho, Nevada, New Mexico, Utah, and Wyoming. That may change in the future as new methods make it more practical to bring geothermal energy to mass-market consumer. "The U.S. Bureau of Land Management says that a dozen Western states could generate 5,500 MW of geothermal energy from 110 plants by 2015, and that number could rise by another 6,600 MW by 2025."[13] But recent funding efforts from the federal government seem to indicate a willingness to back geothermal in much the same way as solar and wind power. As part of the stimulus funding bill, the government aimed $350 million toward developing geothermal energy. The funds will also be used to develop a national geothermal data system and other assorted computer-based support networks for the nationwide geothermal industry. It's hoped that these additional funding mechanisms will really give geothermal the push it needs to stand out from the crowded alternative energy field.

Geothermal careers can range from geologist positions to HVAC installers and contractors who are installing geothermal systems into homes. There are jobs for environmental scientists, geologists, welders, machinists, engineers, administrators, inspectors, contractors, developers, green builders, plumbers, excavators, manufacturers of material for the geothermal energy systems, installers, maintenance technicians, salespeople, and technicians. There are also a whole host of ancillary jobs, including a lot of the building trades people. These jobs are located primarily in Western and Great Plains states, although some geothermal systems are also found in New England. States such as California, Colorado, Utah, and Idaho already have some geothermal operations. In Idaho, a number of state and local government offices are heated and powered by geothermal. The job prospects are positive. Recently, the Bureau of Land Management announced that it was opening leases on 190 million acres of federal land for geothermal projects, "a move that could produce enough clean electricity for 5 million homes."[14] And another study from Iceland predicated that potential U.S. sales of electricity from geothermal sources could reach $29 billion per year. Although, realistically, a $29 billion dollar geothermal industry may be a ways off, these projects show that the government and private industries feel confident enough about the future prospects for geothermal.

Solar Energy

It's amazing to think of how much of the country is awash in sunlight. The vast desert plains of the Southwest rarely see rain, and the Southeast, although it is wet in the summer, averages over 350 sunny days per year. Yet, for all the promises of unlimited power harnessed from the sun, the reality of affordable, compact solar energy has been elusive. That may be changing with advances in solar energy technology. Despite sometimes wavering support, the solar industry has made serious advances over the past decade—both in acceptance at a policy level and in working on bringing costs down enough to make solar energy affordable for citizens and businesses alike.

Photovoltaic cell manufacturers are churning out increasingly advanced systems to harness more and more energy. Solar cells have been unveiled that are thin and that roll out, rather than the bulky, rigid structures so commonly associated with the technology. And even though solar-powered batteries and hot water heaters are commonplace, the solar industry is hoping that solar cells powering homes and businesses will enjoy a similar level of marketplace penetration over the coming years.

Solar energy was last on the nation's radar during the oil crisis of the 1970s. At that time, President Jimmy Carter installed 32 solar hot water panels on the White House roof. It was the government's attempt to set an example for sustainable living, yet the idea of sustainable living was still in its infancy. The solar cells were more geopolitically motivated than anything. Still, it was a bold first move. Next, a bill called the Energy Credits for Individuals was passed in 1980, giving out tax credits for solar, geothermal, and wind power equipment. Companies sprang up to exploit this new-found interest in solar technology.

But, within a few years, oil prices had stabilized, and the solar fad began to diminish in popularity, staying relatively below the radar until recent years, when the new environmental ethos, combined with the awareness of global climate change, brought new skepticism to the fossil fuel industry. President Obama's former green jobs czar, Van Jones, echoed the frustration felt by many in regard to solar energy: "[I]t's ironic that many alternative energies were invented in the U.S., but that European countries are the ones who have taken our ideas and run with them. Germany, for instance, has been successful with solar power and has much less natural sunlight than the majority of the United States."[15] The time is ripe for solar expansion, but some nagging issues remain.

Solar energy may seem like a no-brainer for parts of the country, such as Florida and the Southwest, that enjoy hundreds of days per year bathed in sunshine. As mentioned previously, Florida and other Southern states also go through periods of regular rain during the summer. There are hurricanes and tropical storm issues as well. A company in Wales developed a new cell, made of titanium oxide rather than silicon, which is supposed to be so much more sensitive that indoor solar energy production is possible. If this technology takes off, at least one of the larger technical issues can finally be laid to rest. Right now, the cells are bulky and difficult to work with for residential applications. For the large solar fields you see in pictures dotting the barren landscape of the Southwest desert, the thin roll-out strips of solar cells are not as important. But to the average homeowner, it's going to take that kind of development in cell technology to bring the demand up on the residential side. That does not take into account any commercial businesses that want to go on solar, but it's safe to assume that the better the technology, the greater the demand will be.

Another major stumbling block when you're talking about solar is price. The price is still prohibitively high for most homeowners, leaving conventional applications years away from cost-effective appeal to consumers. The general cost for a fully functioning solar system for an average house of about 2,500 square feet in California is $20,000–30,000.[16] That's an average—not taking into account the variations in costs from different locations, as well as potential credits and tax rebates from states and the federal government. A system for larger homes can exceed $50,000 easily. A better option for a homeowner looking to start small with solar is a solar hot water heater, which is an efficient and effective way to reduce energy consumption.

But back to the jobs. Growth in the field is estimated to be at "more than 30 percent a year for the next five years."[17] With the solar energy industry rising to meet the increasing demand for the systems, the leaders in the solar energy field have emerged in some unlikely places. California is the dominant player in solar installations. The surprising second is the Garden State: "New Jersey is a leading solar energy state, the report noted—with 3,500 residential, commercial and industrial solar energy installations."[18] Solar energy technology manufacturing facilities are found in Arizona, Michigan, Tennessee, and New Mexico. A recent factory that makes photovoltaic tubes as well as cells opened up in New Mexico, illustrating the cutting edge aspects of many of the companies in the solar industry. And the fact that these are manufacturing jobs in the United States is a plus from both an economic impact standpoint and a public relations standpoint for the government.

So the outlook for solar is positive. The naysayers have been getting less and less shrill and more even-opinioned about the solar industry. If government incentives and private investment keep going forward at the current pace, solar will become a ubiquitous part of the landscape. It simply needs to be done. The sun is a constant source of energy that needs to be harnessed as effectively as we can.

Wind Power

Wind power is one of the oldest forms of alternative power generation. There are parts of the world where wind is a large proportion of the energy production. In the United States, swaths of open land in the West and across the Great Plains are beginning to see the growing trend of windmill farms, with the latest bold designs. The picture of a windmill is ubiquitous in alternative energy brochures and reports. (If there's any indication that the rise in interest in wind power is a real move toward an alternative source of power, it has to be the early 2009 crackdown on a Mafia-backed wind farm in Sicily. The mob was laundering money through the farm. You know that when organized crime gets involved, it's no passing fad.)

In terms of alternative energy production, wind is outpacing natural gas in terms of energy produced. The turbines themselves are twice as powerful as they were less than a decade ago, and they will no doubt become even more powerful and efficient in the next decade. That's a big accomplishment, considering that, less than a decade ago, wind was nowhere near having that kind of output. In 2007, wind generated enough kilowatt hours to power over 3 million homes, and the yearly output is expected to increase at a steady pace as new wind turbines are being raised. The increase is expected to be on the order of 20–25 percent yearly. The American Wind Energy Association reported that, in 2009, 85,000 people were employed in the wind energy industry, up an astounding 70 percent from the year before.[19] This bodes well for the industry as a whole. "What's even more encouraging is that U.S. manufacturers . . . accounted for about half of total worldwide small wind turbine sales."[20]

With all these new wind turbines ordered, factories are popping up from Texas to Iowa to meet the growing demand. Even with costs per kilowatt higher than traditional-source power, the demand for wind turbines is growing. Companies are not only building new facilities but renovating older ones. The American Wind Energy Association reported that a Swiss wind turbine manufacturer redeveloped an old U.S. Steel plant in Pennsylvania and turned it into a modern manufacturing facility that won awards for design and brought over 300 jobs to a Rust Belt region. The dominant company in wind power is currently General Electric (GE). But foreign companies are making major inroads into the U.S. wind power scene. Firms such as Siemens and Vestas are bringing hundreds of new jobs to the United States, in part because the United States has such a large share of the global market for wind turbines.

Wind power really got a public relations promotion in 2008 during the record high gas price days. Texas oil tycoon T. Boone Pickens came out with a series of commercials outlining his plan to wean the United States from foreign oil and bring economic development back to the country. His plan was to build a huge wind farm in Texas that was capable of generating enough energy to power over 1.5 million homes. Another interesting part of his plan was to convert all cars to run on compressed natural gas instead of gasoline. In the summer of 2009, Pickens backed off on his original plan, but he indicated that he still wants to become involved in wind power on some level.

Wind has other advantages that could make it more popular with energy-grid managers and public utilities. The industry trade groups say that it will be increasingly easier to merge wind-generated power into the overall energy grid in the United States. With ever more efficient wind turbines, combined with accurate wind forecasting, getting the right amount of energy at the right time on the grid is easier. A greater share of wind power used for electricity puts downward pressure on traditional forms of energy, resulting in an extended lifespan for the oil and coal supplies. That gets back into the earlier point about a combination of energy sources rather than the one-size-fits-all model.

Some people have issues with the expansion of wind power. One so-called fact that is trotted out time and time again by critics of wind power is the deleterious effect that the wind turbines have on bird populations. There have been concerns that bird populations in areas where there are heavy wind turbine coverage are suffering declines as a result of collisions with the turning blades. Studies have found that, although there are some mortalities—associated particularly with older styles of turbines—wind power mortality pales in comparison to other bird mortality causes. Other critics are opposed to the aesthetic impact of wind turbines. These are mainly the ones that are planned for seaside communities, the offshore wind farms, such as the ones that were planned for Martha's Vineyard but then scrapped because people didn't want to look out over the ocean and see giant windmills. The not-in-my-backyard (NIMBY) reaction is a powerful force.

The job outlook for wind power is good, although a lot of it depends on continued support by the U.S. government, especially with a renewable energy policy that levels the field for wind turbines. The wind power job sector added 35,000 positions in 2008, even though the country was in a recession and most job sectors were losing workers. The recession-besting performance may be a fluke, and a lag of unemployment may hit in 2009, but the general trend is upward—with increasing high-paying positions, in addition to wind turbine installers and manufacturing plant workers.

Biofuels

Imagine instead of pulling up to a gas tank and paying the latest high price for a gallon of gas, you pull up behind your local Hooters (famous for deep-fried chicken wings) and hook up a hose to their grease trap. You pump your diesel car full of used vegetable oil and drive away, the fumes accented by the aroma of French fries and chicken wings. Well it's reality for a handful of visionaries who have transformed their old diesel vehicles to work on biodiesel. Even celebrities like Willie Nelson have gotten in on the act. Although biodiesel might not solve all our energy issues, it's a way to reduce dependence on oil as well as using grease—that would normally be disposed of—in a sustainable way.

Biofuel production is an area that has been shown to have great promise from a political perspective but has suffered a lot of popular backlash
from consumers, energy companies, and environmentalists. Specifically,
the use of corn-based ethanol, while supporting a growing labor force,
has been shown to be as much of a product of well-funded subsidies and
political leanings as an actual useful alternative energy. Ethanol is now
up to 10 percent of gasoline, as it is in Florida, and is anticipated to be a
higher share of the nationwide energy picture. Critics charge that
ethanol requires more energy to make than it saves, that it promotes
additional subsidies for the corn industry, and that it is a stop gap for real
fuel change.

The problems associated with corn-based ethanol started with the
manufacturing, which uses a lot of water and actually takes as much
power to produce, by some estimates, as the power it delivers as a fuel.
Then there is the ethical and practical question of utilizing food crops for
energy. Some think that the rising use of food crops for fuel caused a
spike in food prices in 2008, which led to food riots in many countries
around the world. Although the prices have stabilized (and some place
the blame on the changing global climate, coupled with geopolitical considerations), the unease about corn-based ethanol remains.

Ethanol production takes a massive amount of water to work. As
shown in the earlier chapter on water resources, water supply is an over-
riding environmental issue that needs to be addressed. But using water
to make a fuel that has less potential energy than gasoline is not a popular move. In Missouri, citizens sued to stop an ethanol plant "projected
to draw 1.3 million gallons of water a day from the Ozark aquifer."[21]
There are ethanol producers that are working hard to make the corn-
based product more efficient at the manufacturing level. *Forbes* magazine
profiled Poet ethanol, which has reduced the energy needed to produce a
gallon of ethanol by half.

But advanced biofuels—those made of alternative materials such as
switchgrass, straw, cellulose, and other materials—are a rapidly expanding subsector of the biofuels industry. As of early 2009, there were 30
biofuel plants across the country, employing hundreds of workers, many
in rural communities. Plants were located in the following states:
Alabama, California, Colorado, Florida, Georgia, Iowa, Kansas,
Louisiana, Maine, Michigan, Minnesota, Missouri, Montana, Nebraska,
Nevada, New York, Oregon, Pennsylvania, South Carolina, South
Dakota, Tennessee, Wisconsin, and Wyoming.

The jobs range from work in the production of the raw material, primarily in agriculture, to positions for construction workers, engineers,

chemists, plant operators, and managers. Salespeople with a good knowledge of the biofuel business are also in high demand. Established corn ethanol producers are also expanding into the alternative biofuel sector. Companies from Europe have already set up plants in the Midwest to use switchgrass and other plant material to make cellulose-based ethanol. There are entrepreneurs and researchers who are looking to derive biofuels from discarded wood products, vines, weedy plants, and even mulch. It's not certain which of these biofuels will take off, but there will be no shortage of great ideas from innovative start-ups.

Biofuel proponents estimate that direct job creation could account for over 120,000 jobs within the next 10 years, with a multiplier effect bringing that total to over 800,000. Although these numbers are an estimate, they underscore the belief that advanced biofuels can be a real piece of the alternative energy pie, as well as a major green job career path, even though it may be one that is closely aligned with existing manufacturing and processing technology. Another attractive aspect of biofuel plants is that many are located in the Corn Belt and in rural farming areas that do not often attract major industries. The proximity of the plants to the fuel source is important because it reduces the amount of fossil fuels needed to truck the raw material to the plant. This also translates into cost savings for the manufacturing facility and ensures a constant uninterrupted supply of raw material.

There are other potential sources of alternative biofuels: algae for one. Sure the image of green sticky plant material that clings to rocks and blooms in lakes throughout the summer is hardly what one would think of when envisioning a promising new alternative biofuel. But recent scientific advances in processing the algae for biofuel use have made the reality of an algae-based fuel system that much closer to mainstream acceptance. In California alone, there are "nine companies in the San Diego area that are working to develop algae-based substitutes for conventional petroleum products."[22] It might not be too long before you can run to the store with a tank full of green algae.

Education

As mentioned in other chapters, there are far more colleges, universities, and specialized training centers for alternative energy than there is space in this book to list them all. But the following provides a large number of educational options for people looking for a career in alternative energy. Higher educational institutions are adding green career courses and degrees at an increasing pace, sometimes within a few months of coming up with the plan. At Kalamazoo Community College, "the Wind Energy Technology certificate was pushed through in two months, and the certificate of achievement for auto-hybrid and advanced-technology vehicles took three months."[23] A recent report from the Chronicle of Higher Education found that "demand for the degrees in renewable or alternative energy is growing, but schools that offer the degrees remain few and far between."[24]

Some positions, like solar cell installers and wind turbine technicians, are filled by technicians, many of whom already have extensive experience in similar positions. They may not need to go back to school formally, but they may need a little specialized training to complement their existing skills. Training courses are listed under some of these programs and can also be found under the organization's subsection. It's difficult to quantify the number of training programs, because many are held at different times throughout the year and are not part of a specified educational program. State and local governments may be the best source to tap to find out if there are alternative energy training opportunities in your area. Also, community colleges and vocational institutions often offer specialized certificate and degree programs that are aimed at specified technical areas.

- Arizona State University (ASU) School of Sustainability (www.schoolofsustainability.asu.edu). This ASU school is the first one of its kind in the country. Students can choose from certification programs or undergraduate and graduate degree programs in sustainability. The courses represent a wide cross-section of the general environmental field, with other disciplines worked in for an education that's as much hard technical learning as it is a more philosophical approach.
- Arizona University College of Technology and Innovation (technology.asu.edu/engrtech). The College of Technology and Innovation offers one of the few Master's of Science in Technology in alternative energy technologies. Courses concentrate on fuel- and photovoltaic-cell technology.
- Center for Energy and Environmental Studies at Boston University (www.bu.edu/cees). The Center for Energy and Environmental Studies "engages in education, research, and professional training in the fields of energy and environmental analysis." The Center is part of Boston University and offers a variety of undergraduate degrees in conjunction with facilities such as the world-renowned *Woods Hole* Oceanographic

Institute. The Center's three master's degrees are high-level multidisciplinary tracks, bringing together energy, policy, environmental science, and computer technology.

- Center for Sustainable System/University of Michigan (http://css.snre.umich.edu/). The Center is part of the University's School of Natural Resources and the Environment. The Center's focus is on interdisciplinary approaches to sustainability, and it works closely with a variety of government, industry, and citizen stakeholder groups. The university offers an dual degree in Engineering Sustainable Systems.
- Center of Excellence for Energy Technology/Washington (www.centralia.edu). The Center is a self-described research hub in Washington State, for students looking to get degrees in energy technology. The Center is designed to serve as a one-stop shop where a prospective student can look for colleges in Washington that offer a variety of energy degrees, from associate's to master's, in energy-related fields. Many of these certificate programs are in conjunction with employers, allowing the Center to help graduates find employment with energy companies in the Northwest. The other useful feature is a list of apprenticeships for students looking to get trade instruction. These apprenticeships range from electrical contractors to line workers.
- Central Carolina Community College/North Carolina (www.cccc.edu/biofuels/). In 2008, this community college in North Carolina began offering an associate's degree in Alternative Energy Technology with a concentration in Biofuels. The college is currently working on a widescale research project to develop new biofuels from common feedstock.
- Cloud County Community College/Kansas (www.cloud.edu). Cloud County offers one of the only wind energy technology associate's degree programs in the country. There is also a certificate degree. Both programs are designed to train displaced professionals and new students to supplement Kansas's growing wind power industry.
- Coconino Community College/Arizona (www.ccsedi.org/). This small community college in Arizona is part of the Coconino County Sustainable Economic Development Initiative. It offers an associate's degree in Applied Science in Alternative Energy, specializing in solar technology and installation. It also offers classes in green building and alternative design.

- Columbia Gorge Community College/Oregon (www
  .cgcc.cc.or.us). The Columbia Gorge's renewable energy program, concentrating on wind technology, offers a 1-year certificate and 2-year Associate of Applied Science degree. The
  college's program is regarded highly in the industry.
- Consortium for Education in Renewable Energy Technology/
  Madison Area Technical College, Wisconsin (www.ceret.us).
  In 2005, the College received a grant from the National
  Science Foundation to further develop existing 2-year college
  technical programs focusing on renewable energy by bringing
  in experts in the field to teach practical courses to complement
  the existing curriculums. Graduates receive a Renewable
  Energy Certificate. The consortium has expanded the program to other colleges. Courses (both online and classroom-
  based) include Introduction to Hybrid Electric Vehicles,
  Introduction to Wind Energy, Introduction to Biofuels, Basic
  Photovoltaic System Site Assessment, and over a dozen more
  courses.
- Crowder College's Missouri Alternative and Renewable Technology Center (www.crowder.edu/MARET/). It might not be
  one of the larger universities, but Crowder College offers associate degrees in solar energy, wind energy, and biofuels and
  works with the University of Missouri on the Center's research
  programs. The college is constructing a new building to house
  the Center, using the latest green building methods.
- Evergreen Institute (www.evergreeninstitute.org). The Institute's Center for Renewable Energy and Green Building, headquartered in Colorado, offers courses and certificates in
  residential green building and residential renewable energy.
- Heatspring Learning Institute (www.heatspring.com). Heatspring is a private educational company that holds training sessions in solar and geothermal energy. The courses are designed
  for entry-level employees through "building designers and system installers." The company also consults a Technical Advi-
  sory Board to ensure the quality of the courses.
- Highland Community College/Illinois (www.highland.cc.il.us).
  This community college offers a unique wind turbine technician
  training program. The program offers an associate's degree in
  applied science and a turbine technician certificate.
- Mid-State Technical College/Wisconsin (www.mstc.edu/index
  .htm). Mid-State offers associate degrees in biorefinery

technologies, renewable energy, renewable electricity, renewable
thermal energy, and energy efficiency.

- Oregon Institute of Technology (OIT) (www.oit.edu/
  renewableenergy). OIT developed its 4-year undergraduate
  degree program in renewable energy in 2005. It was the first
  of its kind in the country. The campus is geothermally heated
  (the only such campus in the United States, so the Institute
  takes its alternative energy seriously. The program is
  designed around an engineering track, with strong emphasis
  on math and physics.
- San Juan College/New Mexico (www.sanjuancollege.edu). The
  Southwest seems a perfect place to train students in solar installation and design. It's no wonder that so many of the certification programs are located here. San Juan College offers both a
  1-year and 2-year degree in Photovoltaic System Design and
  Installation.
- State University of New York (SUNY) at Canton (www.canton
  .edu/csoet/alt_energy/). The Canton campus of SUNY offers a
  degree in alternative and renewable energy systems from wind
  to solar to biofuels. The comprehensive major concentrates on
  engineering and math.
- Training4Green (www.training4green.com). This institute
  offers the ultimate in environmentally friendly learning—online
  courses in solar business and photovoltaic-cell technology. Based
  in California, the two career paths are the only training courses
  for now, and the company's courses are accredited by the Dis-
  tance Education and Training Council.
- University of Idaho Biodiesel education (www.uiweb.uidaho
  .edu/bioenergy/). Students can get an education in biodiesel
  through the university's department of Biological & Agricultural Engineering. The University operates this education site
  with assistance from the U.S. Department of Agriculture.
- University of Illinois Center for Advanced BioEnergy Research
  (www.bioenergy.illinois.edu/). As part of a university-wide
  cooperative education effort, the Center runs training programs
  and research on emerging areas of bioenergy. The Center also
  runs a blog, with daily updates on the world of biofuels and
  alternative energy from biological sources. Beginning in 2009,
  the university will offer a master's degree in bioenergy.
- University of Massachusetts at Amherst/Center for Energy
  Efficient & Renewable Energy (www.ceere.org). As part of the

University's College of Engineering, the Center offers training in real-life alternative energy issues and applications for under-graduate and graduate students. The Center partners with gov-ernment and private stakeholders and conducts extensive research into a variety of clean energy solutions.

- University of Wisconsin at Madison/Solar Energy Laboratory (http://sel.me.wisc.edu/). This lab is the oldest in the country for researching and developing new ways to harness solar energy and practical methods for making solar energy more widely available. The lab works with the engineering depart-ment and allows students in mechanical and chemical engineer-ing programs to add a solar component to their coursework, positioning them for jobs in the solar power industry at a higher job level.

Job Resources

Many of the general environmental job Web sites mentioned in Chapter 2 have listings of available alternative energy positions. The fol-lowing are job resources that focus exclusively on alternative energy. Also featured are some representative companies that are leading the charge to make alternative energy a viable business enterprise. Other major corpo-rations, such as GE and BP, also have job openings in alternative energy. But the following ones are more niche-oriented. The larger corporations have well-staffed human resources departments, and it would be best to contact them directly or look up job availability online.

- Algenol (www.algenolbiofuels.com). This algae biofuel company is headquartered in Florida and is on the cutting edge of using algae for biofuel production.
- Alternative Energy Jobs (www.alternativeenergy.com/jobs). It's exactly what the name says, an overall site for alternative energy jobs. The site offers a blog, chat room, job hunting group to discuss strategies with other seekers, news section, and alter-native energy products for sale.
- Alternative Energy News (www.alternative-energy-news.com). This site is a news outlet for issues relating to all alternative energies, from solar to biofuels to hydrogen. The site also has a green jobs board, in addition to event listings and a link to all the social networking sites on which Alternative Energy News has a presence.

- Careers in Wind (www.jobtarget.com/home/index.cfm ?site_id=770). This full-service job board offers positions in wind energy. It allows users to create specific profiles for themselves and save setting for job searches.
- Clean Edge Jobs (jobs.cleanedge.com/). This is a straightforward, no-nonsense job board, mainly for private companies looking for interns and paid employees. There are also some helpful articles, a number of reports on various clean technologies, and a summit scheduled for 2010 to bring together business representatives and investors for clean technology companies.
- Cool Climate Jobs (www.coolclimatejobs.com/). This job site specializes in positions relating to climate change: consultants, economists, educators, journalists, and scientists. The jobs are located worldwide and are primarily for NGOs and academia.
- Energy Crossing (www.energycrossing.com/). Part of the Employment Crossing Web site, this section lets jobs seekers see what states have jobs in green energy and pick through a variety of career types.
- Energy Experts (www.energyexperts.org). This site specializes in alternative energy position in California and the Pacific Northwest, including Alaska. It also offers links to training and education resources.
- Fuel Cells 2000 (www.fuelcells.org). A general site for everything relating to fuel-cell technologies, it lists available job positions, internship opportunities, and professional development trainings and certificate programs.
- Geothermal Energy Association (GEA) (www.geo-energy.org). A trade organization for professionals in the field, the GEA is also a great resource for job opportunities in geothermal as well as the latest developments in the field and in areas of the country that are looking at starting up geothermal energy projects.
- Green Energy Jobs (www.greenenergyjobs.com/). The name says it all. Green Energy jobs lists hundreds of positions in the usual fields, as well as wave energy, carbon trading, finance, waste management, and bioenergy. The Web site also offers sectors updates giving some thoughts on trends in the various alternative energy fields.
- Green Energy Jobs Online (www.greenenergyjobsonline.com/). Slightly different than the prior Web site, this is one of the

Energy Job Sites. It has a useful tool for looking at company locations across the globe and lists jobs for seekers, as well as offering listings for employers.

- Green Energy One-Stop (www.green-solar-wind-hydrogen -energy.com/). A comprehensive alternative energy site, Green Energy One-Stop offers a wealth of information on the latest developments in alternative energy businesses, as well as legislation relating to energy issues, relayed mainly through links to other sites, as well as product lines and green job boards.
- Green Tech Media (www.greentechmedia.com). As alternative energy becomes more and more a matter of national policy and focus, sites like GreenTechMedia are more important. It's a comprehensive multimedia, "integrated online-media company comprised of cutting-edge news, in-depth market research, and focused industry events." Combining top-shelf journalism with policy analysis, business advice, and career information, the site is one of the leading sources of alternative energy information.
- Horizon Wind Energy (www.horizonwind.com). A Texas-based wind energy company, with branch offices in locations from Washington to New York, the site lists job opportunities with the company as well as internships.
- Hydrogen Fuel Cells Jobs Board (www.hydrogenassociation .org/jobs/). The National Hydrogen Association's main Web site has this page, specifically dedicated to positions in the hydrogen and fuel-cell technology field. Job seekers can create profiles and search through the jobs board, and employers looking for new talent can recruit through the same site.
- Hydropower Research Foundation (www.hydrofoundation.org). A research organization dedicated to hydropower, this Web site has a job board, internship list, and schedule of upcoming events in the hydropower industry.
- My Green Education (www.mygreeneducation.com). This Web site focuses on green training and education opportunities in all areas of green technology and science, but primarily alternative energy. The site has a job board, as well as links to education options and certification programs.
- My Green Scene (www.mygreenscene.com). This is a comprehensive renewable energy site, highlighting training programs, grant opportunities, business ventures, and, of course, job openings in renewable energy. There are also articles about

investing in green energy companies and information on green building and how it ties in with energy efficiency and renewable sources.

- National Renewable Energy Laboratory (www.nrel.gov/). Located in Colorado, the National Renewable Lab works on cutting-edge products and application for alternative energy. The site has job opportunities at the lab and at associated research institutions.
- Renewable Energy Jobs (www.renewableenergyjobs.com/). A straightforward job Web site with national and international listings of green energy jobs. The positions fall across all categories, even office and administrative jobs.
- Renewable Energy World (www.renewableenergyworld.com/rea/home). This Web site is dedicated to renewable energy with news, jobs, products, finance, and video feeds. It's a great general resource for information on the various forms of energy, and the job board is fairly comprehensive.
- Solar Jobs (www.solarjobs.com/). Like the wind power job site that follows, this one is solely directed at bringing together qualified candidates in solar technology and firms and agencies looking to hire. The site acts as more of a headhunter than most and places job seekers in positions ranging from accounting to manufacturing to engineering.
- Sustain Jobs (www.sustainjobs.com/). This sleek, modern site lists sustainability and renewable energy jobs from academia, government, finance, law, and major global corporations. The jobs are located across the globe. The site also lists upcoming energy conferences and training events.
- Wind Industry Jobs (www.windindustryjobs.com). This is a really comprehensive Web site for wind energy. In addition to jobs in various wind-energy sectors, the site lists industry recruiters that can be useful for would-be wind technicians. Users can create a profile and keep a tally on jobs they search and apply for.

Associations/Organizations/General Resources

- Alliance to Save Energy (ase.org). This is a comprehensive resource site covering a broad range of energy efficiency topics, legislative matters, changing regulations regarding energy efficiency, and links to a variety of alternative energy organizations

across the globe. The site also links to open green energy
careers.

- American Council for an Energy Efficient Economy
  (www.aceee.org). This organization advocates for "policies to
  improve energy efficiency can reduce oil imports, improve the
  reliability of the U.S. electric grid, save consumers money,
  reduce air pollution, create jobs, and reduce prices." The site also
  has a comprehensive job board and various publications dealing
  with energy efficiency.
- American Solar Energy Society (www.ases.org). Started way
  back in 1954, this organization is dedicated to advancing the
  usage of solar-based technologies. Current membership numbers around 12,000, with chapters in over 40 states. The Society
  runs an annual solar conference, hosts seminars, offers networking opportunities, publishes a magazine, supports grass
  root solar power efforts, and a has a number of other programs
  dedicated to solar.
- Association of Energy Engineers (www.aeecenter.org). With
  over 70 countries represented, this organization of engineers
  promotes sustainable development and has an active education
  component offering certifications, conferences, seminars, and
  Web seminars. There is also a job board link to the Energy Vor-
  tex career center.
- Database of State Incentives for Renewables and Efficiency
  (www.dsireusa.org). Begun in 1995, this project from the
  North Carolina Solar Center, the Interstate Renewable Energy
  Council, and the U.S. Department of Energy tracks all the federal, state, and local financial incentives, laws, and policies
  regarding the use of renewable energy and energy efficiency in
  building.
- Energy Bible (www.energybible.com). The Energy Bible Web
  site covers all the major renewable energy topics in great detail
  and has regularly updated features on the various types of alternative energy. It also lists various companies working the
  respective fields. The Web site stands out, with a section on
  spiritual energy that includes commentary from philosophers,
  religious leaders, and ethicists.
- Geothermal Energy Association (www.geo-energy.org). This is
  a trade association advocating the use and expansion of geothermal energy. It hosts an annual conference and various networking events and workshops.

- Solar Energy Industries Association (www.seia.org). This advocacy organization works to improve outreach and education about solar energy technology and works with lawmakers at state and federal levels to open up the marketplace for solar energy companies. The organization holds various events, including a national conference.

CHAPTER 5

BUILDING FOR THE FUTURE

Green building is the concept of building a structure designed to maximize energy efficiency and water consumption, reduce indoor air pollutants, maximize use of recyclable building materials, reduce waste and pollution, reduce environmental impacts, and reduce operating expenses. It could be any combination of the previous ideas, but the common thread is sustainability. But the variations in what exactly constitutes a green building have led to certifications and guidelines for materials, methods, and ways of building for a project to be truly called green.

Some of the concepts in alternative energy—greater efficiency, less dependence on traditional energy sources, greater flexibility and choice—are also cornerstones of the green building mantra. Low-impact development (LID), green building, Leadership in Energy and Environmental Design (LEED) certification, sustainable development—these are all buzzwords for a new way to look at home building, architecture, landscaping, and living. From city planners to your neighborhood tree trimmer, the future of building and development has opened up new avenues for the green-minded.

Green building was gaining momentum before the real estate crash of the mid-2000s, but, even as the real estate market cooled to almost stagnant levels, the concept of building greener has not only remained but is gaining even more clout. Recently, the owners of the Sears Tower (now the Willis Tower) in Chicago announced a $350 million dollar project to "cut electricity use by 80 percent and construct a net-zero energy luxury hotel next door."[1] In green-minded countries such as India, green building has also taken hold, with projects appearing on a regular basis. And green building is not relegated to new developments either. It's estimated that retrofitting and redeveloping existing buildings using green methods "would result in an estimated savings of $160 billion in energy costs, while creating green jobs that can't be exported."[2]

Federal support for green building is seen throughout the 2009 stimulus package. Among the various spending proposals that made it to the final version was $5 billion for assistance to low-income families to weatherize their homes and improve energy efficiency. There was over $3 billion for rehabbing and modernizing public housing developments, including making them more energy-efficient. There were also provisions that new federal buildings would have to be made with green building in mind. There's no real estimate on how many federal facilities will be certified as green buildings, but there is at least a feeling that the federal government is not just making talk with this idea. Even though energy prices are rising, it makes sense to set a course to use federal resources more effectively, which, as everyone knows, is often the antithesis of how the government usually works!

The recent cap-and-trade debates (discussed in Chapter 8 on Green Law) are bringing changes to building codes at both local and federal levels. There is a move for "all states move to adopt standards for residential and commercial structures that are at least 30 percent better than two widely accepted energy codes."[3]

Green building is certainly at an important junction in its acceptance by the mainstream, both consumers and developers. As one expert in the field, Elie Araj, commented, "There's no reason why green building should not be the norm. It is only a question of critical mass and the economy at this point. Some of the products and 'knowledge' is still concentrated in the hands of a few, thus controlling supply and stifling demand. As more products are introduced and the knowledge base widens (both on the user and provider) then the integration in construction/design would be imminent."[4]

With all the push for green building and the growing enthusiasm for green projects, there was a question of exactly how to categorize a green building. There was a need for a way to address the issues of how sustainable certain building materials were and whether certain types of insulation and energy saving devices were as efficient and added to the overall green ethos of the project. A certification program could be a way to ensure that all builders who chose to have their building qualify as green would have a set of criteria to follow.

This idea of a certification method for ensuring that buildings adhered to a set of rules and criteria for green design was the driving force behind the formation of the LEED program. In 1998, LEED was introduced by the U.S. Green Building Council (USGBC) as a way to promote the idea of energy-efficient designs in buildings and incorporate the ideas of sustainable development in community planning. LEED certification expanded to include structures from commercial buildings to sports arenas. In 2008, LEED for Homes was introduced. In fact, the founder of the USGBC moved into a LEED Platinum-certified home, the highest rating available.

With LEED quickly gaining acceptance across the building community, planners, architects, contractors, and consultants raced into the fold to become LEED-certified. It became a marketing item—not only for people looking to work on green building projects, but for the projects themselves. Advertising their office building as a LEED-certified building could lead to higher demand from certain segments of the business community, and the same concept applies to home buyers.

In 2009, the LEED exam was revamped to reflect the current trends in green building. It's anticipated that this will not be the last adjustment of the standards. As each new technology emerges and as methods of green building become more refined, it will be imperative for the LEED standards to keep up with the changes. Rather than constraining the application of green building techniques, LEED standards are driving the industry to adapt and change the way buildings are designed and constructed.

Another side effect of a LEED certification or other green building certification is a marketing cache. Here is another area where green marketing dovetails with actual, in-the-field practices. Many LEED buildings aggressively advertise their LEED status and energy efficiency. Rather than being looked at as a cheap marketing ploy, people are beginning to understand that the certification reflects a true commitment to green policies. Hotels have begun their own green certification programs, and it's not uncommon to find the a hotel touting its green credentials. Although these certification programs may not have the same rigorous standards as more well-known programs, they do result in less energy usage, coupled with the increased marketing cache.

There is an increase in cost associated with LEED compliance, leaving some contractors to find other ways to stay green without necessarily going the LEED route. According to William Tuyn, director of town planning for engineering firm GPI, "In fact the National Association of Home Builders (NAHB) resistance to the increased cost represented by

compliance with LEED standards and application for LEED certification
has resulted in that organization's creation of its own 'Green Building'
program. In cooperation with the International Code Council (ICC),
NAHB now runs its own Certified Green Professional accreditation
program."[5]

The Rocky Mountain Institute stated that "many developers fear that
following a green agenda will delay project schedules and raise
costs. ... The reality, however, is that well-executed green development
projects ... perform extremely well financially. In fact, even though
many of the leading-edge developers ... have strong environmental
backgrounds and ideals, the financial rewards of green development are
now bringing mainstream developers into the fold at an increasing
pace."[6]

In fact, many developers see green building as a way to stand out in a
crowded field—not only during the economic downturn, but when
development and real estate are in a boom cycle. Professionals in the
field, such as Elie Araj, are now seeing a shift in attitudes "not only more
than 5–10 years ago, more than a year ago. Some developers did not want
to even discuss this stuff. Now they see me, and they are like: You know
all this green building stuff, I think it makes sense if . . . so they are now
more engaged in the debate."[7]

In response to the Energy Independence and Security Act of 2007, the
Department of Energy set up the High-Performance Commercial Green
Building Partnership, to provide technical guidance to the Department.
The Partnership is made up of industry representatives, including architects, HVAC professionals, and the USGBC. They are tasked with guid-
ing the future of green building design and how it will take shape in the
coming years.

The USGBC has also reevaluated its mission and expanded its critical
support areas where their leadership on issues is needed. The USGBC is
now a well-known name, and the LEED certification is a respected and
desired commodity. The Council has spoken out vociferously in favor of
additional funding for green building training at the state and federal
government levels. It outlined the need for the additional professionals in
the field to cope with the expected increase in green building projects.
The Council also tasked the government to lead by example and to
make the design and construction of government buildings green. LEED
certifications for government buildings and schools are a fast-growing
segment of the LEED process. Another activist role that the USGBC
takes is promoting education and training opportunities for professionals in the field, as well as giving support to green job training programs

by helping the teachers in those programs with the expertise of the Council and its members.

One other direct area in which the USGBC wants to have influence is in the promotion of making affordable housing green. With the current cost of many recyclable materials and other parts of green building, that may no longer be a cost-effective strategy, but the Council believes that offering a chance for green living to people other than the upper crust of the economic ladder makes perfect business sense and is yet another way to get the word out about green building. Plus, it's thought that the increased energy efficiency will be an economic boon to the owners, giving them more economic clout in the greater community. The less they are spending on their electricity bill each month, the more they have for groceries, food, and so on. Finally the USGBC is supporting the creation of a revolving loan fund, similar to clean water revolving funds, that lends money to state and local governments at low interest rates for use in green building projects. The idea could be coupled with an increase in direct government funding of green building projects. The one-two punch of financial incentives and direct investment could jump-start the building boom and bring in an extra value-added aspect to the developments.

Green building is, in a sense, about getting back to traditional ways of building, rather than subscribing to homes that are, in the words of author and lyricist Neil Peart, "detached and subdivided in the mass production zone." Green building offers the chance to embrace new development concepts that echo the old way in which towns were laid out and yet suggest newer development designs that are geared toward maximizing both the available natural resources and the potential profit to the developer. In fact, green building ties into new development through various development types, including new urbanism and LID. These concepts are driving a lot of ideas in green building and are transforming new developments into models of manageable, effective urban living, as well as suburban sprawl, with an eye toward environmental sustainability. Sustainable development is an idea that's championed by groups such as the Foundation for Sustainable Development as ways that poor, Third World countries can bring about economic growth while maintaining the integrity of their natural resources. This type of grass-roots effort is taking hold in many parts of the world and is championed, to some extent, by activists in the United States who view this as a way for poor rural towns to grow into prosperity.

The idea of new urbanism is a development strategy that has been coming into vogue over the past decade. The idea is that by building close-knit, walkable communities, people will once again be drawn to a downtown-living style, rather than suburban sprawl. Communities in cities from Annapolis, Maryland, to Tampa, Florida, have embraced this development concept: street-front businesses, with parking in the back; businesses on the ground floor, with living areas on top; tightly packed residences; large swaths of open space; access to mass transit; and a sustainable set of businesses, to allow for more walking than driving. This style of living falls into a more cultural milieu, but there are definite environmental benefits. In new urbanism developments, drainage design usually allows for infiltration and treatment of stormwater, rather than simply funneling water down curb and gutter systems into the nearest water body. These developments may also be redevelopment of formerly undesirable areas, such as brownfields. Using these developed tracts to bring new life to a community falls squarely into the sustainability ethos of many environmental organizations and green building coalitions.

LID is a concept that goes beyond new urbanism and is more driven by environmental concerns. In most of the country, including Florida, LID is mainly driven by water-resource protection and is a cornerstone of treating stormwater runoff and minimizing flow velocity during storm events. Both of these tasks preserve water quality, as well as dealing with issues relating to a quick and sudden abundance of water quantity. The idea is to build developments, even sprawled subdivisions, with clustered homes and swaths of open space for infiltration of rain water and conservation of wetlands and uplands. LID extends to commercial buildings in the development, utilizing ideas such as permeable pavement and grassed medians in parking lots, to vegetated swale systems instead of sidewalks in areas of the development where people simply don't walk. A well-designed LID system takes into account the predevelopment hydrology of the area, the types of soils, the topography, the wildlife, the vegetative makeup of the site, and any particular permit or regulatory issues. For example, LID is being looked at by the Florida Department of Environmental Protection as a way to address TMDL issues. The ideas and innovation involved in LID are going to challenge a whole new group of green building professionals, as increased regulations regarding development and water quality become more commonplace.

Green roofs are another interesting part of green building that combines the expertise of landscape architects with stormwater and civil engineering. The basic idea is that, when a roof of vegetation is planted, stormwater is captured and infiltrated into the green design—it is not all running down the building and causing runoff. Also, the green building reduces energy consumption by keeping the building cooler during the hot summer months. The green roof concept has taken off in many communities across North America, including Chicago and Toronto. Although still in its infancy, the idea that green roofs will be the norm in urban cores is not unrealistic. As the expertise in making these roof increases and the materials needed to make them become more affordable, the economic and environmental benefits will attract more businesses and governments to the concept.

Another intriguing green concept has been pushed by the city of Chicago. Its Green Alleys program was a way to make green byways out of the often unsightly alleyways that snake through the city's neighborhoods, reducing the impervious surface. The city's transportation department used green techniques and materials, including "recycled construction materials, permeable pavement, recycled rubber sidewalks,"[8] as well as efforts to clean up the alleys and make them not only more functional but aesthetically pleasing, or as pleasing as an alley could possibly be. Between the program's inception in 2006 and 2008, the city installed 80 green alleys.

The outlook for green building jobs is positive, even with setbacks such as the real estate meltdown. For all the doom and gloom, things will start back on a recovery track, and green building is poised to be more at the front of the new wave of building and redevelopment than it was previously. As mentioned earlier, part of the reason that green building may have a stronger presence is as a result of government backing and incentives. These tax breaks and credits, according to William Tuyn, "will increase desirability for the consumer who will then choose to include green options in their new home and home improvement budgets. Ultimately this will result in an increase the number of contractors who adapt to meet market demand."[9] And even though up-front costs of green building construction are still high and the long-term cost savings are still not quite there, the continuing popularity of green buildings will bring down those costs as more and more companies enter the green materials marketplace and technology improves to lower the costs and really drive home (no pun intended) the savings. Knowledge of the full picture of green building, in the words of journalist M. W. Avera, "will likely result in more satisfied customers and the faster evolution of green products."[10]

Types of Jobs

Green building covers a lot of job categories—from contractors to laborers to HV/AC to architects. The construction industry, as of the writing of this book, is going through a prolonged slowdown. But things will eventually recover. This is the time for construction professionals, as well as developers, to learn all they can about LEED. As previously mentioned, the fear is that there will be a dearth of trained professionals available for green building contractors when the jobs come.

Energy efficiency is a cornerstone of green building that dates back prior to this latest trend. In the past, high costs have kept a lot of the more innovative practices off-limits for mass production. But with the green building concept gaining ground, there is a need for workers to retrofit older buildings to new, green standards, as well as those workers needed to build cutting-edge homes and residential complexes.

LEED-certified professionals have become invaluable assets in both the private and public sector. In a recent *Wall Street Journal* article, green builders lamented a shortage of people who were adept at doing it.[11] It's becoming easier for people interested in the training to get the materials, attend online review sessions, and take the test. There is a cost consideration, because the investment can be fairly substantial, depending on what level of involvement the person wants (e.g., buy review materials, attend review classes). However, the certification is one of those résumé builders that can only enhance a prospective job seeker's chances with a company.

Sarasota County, Florida, has made LID a cornerstone of its land and growth management. Florida has never been known to be on the forefront of any kind of progressive growth management, letting unrestrained sprawl go on unencumbered. But decades of poor management have left a parched landscape and residents weary of overburdened infrastructure. One of the benefits of LID in an area like Sarasota is maximizing the infiltration of rainwater to replenish the aquifer while, at the same time, allowing the stormwater to filter through natural mediums, reducing stormwater runoff pollution. Here professionals are called on to design LID structures and landscaping plans.

Landscape architecture is also a growing field that ties in closely with professionals in green building and development systems such as new urbanism and LID. Landscape architects are not just people who simply decide where the plants go. Says Pat Millington, "Landscape does not mean plants, it means the bigger picture, the place as a whole."[12] Landscape architects can therefore be essential in bringing together the vision of the building architect with that of the developer and the engineer. Adds Millington, "As big picture thinkers, we cannot simply focus on small details, we are always looking for how things interact/fit/work with one another."[13] The one advantage that students looking to get into the field have is that there aren't many people who are aware of what landscape architects do, yet the demand is increasing. That's always the best position to be in for a potential job seeker according to Millington: "Until people understand and are familiar with our field, there will still be too few landscape architects."[14]

Another green building career avenue is planning. Planning departments in municipal governments across the country are embracing ideas of sustainability and new urbanism as cornerstones of zoning regulations, transportation plans, and long-term comprehensive land use plans. Careers in planning are often in the public sector, at government agencies. These jobs can pay well, especially in larger urban environments, where innovative thinking for rehabilitating and redeveloping aging urban cores is needed. In some urban centers, planning organizations, using public feedback through targeted charettes (collaboration on an issue among stakeholders), are working toward the overall improvement of the citizen's quality of life. In Philadelphia, there is a project to create a "long-term, sustainable roadmap for using, acquiring, developing, funding, and managing open space in our city's neighborhoods."[15]

Another area of green building employment is consulting companies that specialize in green design and engineering. Positions in these firms can range from land use planners to water-resource and civil engineers. Consulting firms are usually the drivers behind working with regulators and politicians to adjust land use regulations to fit new urbanism and LID projects. These firms can usually attract top-shelf talent, even drawing from municipal governments. Although the consulting industry was hit hard by the downturn in real estate in the mid-2000s, the future of green building and the lack of LEED-certified consultants and engineers could make this job track very attractive for someone coming out of school or already in the construction industry and working toward LEED certification.

General Resources/Organizations

- Building Green (www.buildinggreen.com). This Web site has case studies, manufacturer links for green building products, essential green building concepts, LEED information, and updated news stories relating to green building.
- Global Green Property Services (www.globalgreenps.com/). This unique site is a clearinghouse for vendors and suppliers of green products, many designed for use in green building applications. Although it is not a job site, nor one for retail sales of green products, this is a good site to get a feel for the companies out there who are making the actual green products.

- Green Communities (www.greencommunitiesonline.org). This is a 5-year project to build over 8,000 sustainable, affordable houses using green building criteria. This is a public-private partnership and gives a broad overview of the types of projects that a person in green building can be involved with, from the planning stage to construction.
- Greener Buildings (greenerbuildings.com/). It's an in-depth site with resources, articles, discussions, and blogs in a variety of green building topics, from materials to design to construction.
- The Low Impact Development Center, Inc. (www.lowimpactdevelopment.org). The LID Center is an advocate for integrating LID concepts into zoning and land use planning. The goal is geared toward maintaining hydrologic flow and water quality. The Center offers 1- and 2-day workshops on LID, as well as a variety of publications and resources on the topic.
- Smart Growth Online (www.smartgrowth.org). A Web site with a large amount of resources and information on smart-growth policies, theories, case studies, and networking links.
- Sustainable Architecture, Building, and Culture (www.sustainableabc.com). If you have a beautiful Victorian home that you renovated with energy-efficient appliances, a solar water heater, rain barrels, and eco-friendly landscaping, this site is a place to list your home if it's for sale. That's one of many unique features of this site dedicated to all things sustainable about real estate.

Education/Trainings

In June 2009, The John D. and Catherine T. MacArthur Foundation dedicated an additional $7.6 million, for a combined total of $15 million in grants, for 15 universities across the globe, to develop a master's degree in Development Practice, with an emphasis on sustainable development. The first university to develop the program is Columbia University in New York City. It was the latest push for more formal education for aspects of green building, especially from the development sector.

- Ecoscaper Certification Program: Wild Ones (www.wildcertification.org/ecoscaper). This certification is designed for landscape architects and landscaping professionals to become familiar with green landscaping techniques and native plant communities. To go through the three levels of this certification program, successful applicants must complete a test and do fieldwork projects at each level before passing the course. The training must be accomplished within a 2-year period. After certification, there is an annual renewal certification process.

- Cornell University/Landscape Architecture (courses.cuinfo.cornell.edu/CoScourses.php?college=ALS&dept=Landscape+Architecture). Cornell is one of many schools that has a landscape architecture program. You can find others at www.uscollegesearch.org/landscape-architecture-colleges.html.
- Green Building (www.greenbuilding.com/). The Green Advantage® certification was designed for builders, contractors, and tradespeople in the construction and remodeling industries. Although not as well-known as the LEED certification program, the Green Advantage® program is an up-and-coming certification, with growing name recognition
- Green Building Professional Training (www.builditgreen.org). This organization has the Certified Green Building Professional certification. It's only open to California building professionals. Upon completion of the training, the professional's name is placed in a database that the public can access when looking for certified green builders.
- Green Futures Research and Design Lab/University of Washington (www.greenfutures.washington.edu). The Lab is part of the university's College of Architecture and Urban Planning. The Lab integrates green building concepts with landscape architecture, urban planning, traditional architecture, and green infrastructure. The Lab also partners with nearby community groups and local governments for hands-on research projects.
- Green Plumbers USA (www.greenplumbersusa.com). The Green Plumbers is a national accreditation and training program designed to educate plumbing professionals on topics such as water conservation, solar-powered water tanks, and use of sustainable materials in plumbing construction and repair. It's a 32-hour, five-course program based in California, but it is available to select other states. The information to request a workshop is on the Web site.

- Green Roofs for Healthy Cities (www.greenroofs.org). The Green Roofs program offers an accreditation program of coursework, followed by a comprehensive exam. Like other licensed professionals, continuing education hours are needed to keep current on the certification. Trainings are held in various U.S. cities, as well as in Canada.
- Pervious Pavement Certification (www.nrmca.org). This certification program is run through the National Ready Mixed Concrete Association. The training certifies that the applicant of pervious pavement is knowledgeable on the unique features of permeable concrete and can install it to specifications. The certification is dependent on the passing of a comprehensive examination and is renewable every 5 years.
- U.S. Green Building Council (www.usgbc.org/). The USGBC is a trade organization that developed the LEED system for rating green buildings in 2000. The Council offers extensive training opportunities, as well as certification as a LEED professional. All the information needed for the LEED courses is contained on the site. This should be the first stop for anyone interested in green building.

Job Resources

Green building categories can be found on many of the major job sites, such as Careerbuilder, Job Monkey, Monster, and Simplyhired. The following are sites specifically concentrating on the unique aspects of green building.

But for those looking to get into green building, traditional avenues of entrance into the construction industry are also an opportunity to get a foot in the door with a developer or construction company. Getting a job in the construction industry is another animal, in terms of how to go about getting experience and learning the trade, that is not within the scope of this book. But traditional construction activities are always an option. With that basic background, many local and state agencies, as well as NGOs, offer job training programs to learn methods for green building. Some contractors also train their employees as they move into green building.

- American Planning Association (APA) (www.planning.org). The APA is the nation's largest planning professional organization. The Web site also has links to jobs, as well as helpful hints in planning for job seekers. Because green planning is tied in so close to the traditional planning careers, it's a good idea to read through all the available positions to see how many contain green aspects or can morph into green jobs.

- Green Building Jobs (www.greenbuildingjobs.net). Flexibility is the key here. You can choose from freelance, temporary, and permanent positions, from worldwide companies and from positions across the green building spectrum. The job categories get very specific. Some examples are the following: green building positions in school construction, green information technology and infrastructure, construction accounting services, and lighting supplies.

- Organic Architect (www.organicarchitect.com/consulting/). This San Francisco-based green architecture firm is an example of the types of companies that a landscape or a LEED-certified architect can work for. The company offers design services, as well as consulting for green building projects. Being LEED-certified gives them, as it would any architect, a leg up on dealing with customers looking for sustainable practices and design.

- Top Building Jobs (www.topbuildingjobs.com). It's a general building Web site for job seekers and employers in commercial and residential construction, from developers to vendors and building supply companies. The site also lists green building job openings.

- U.S. Green Building Council Career Center (careercenter .usgbc.org). Part of the USGBC Web site is devoted to green jobs. The site is split in half between job seekers and potential employers. Jobs range from public to private sector; there are also some internships mixed in with the regular positions. The board concentrates mainly on green building jobs.

CHAPTER 6

GREEN BUSINESS

What better way is there to illustrate how pervasive green business practices have become than with beer? Beer is a product that uses a tremendous
amount of water, both in the product itself and in the various processes
needed to come up with the finished lager, ale, porter, and so on. Sustainability has crept into the industry in the form of organically produced
beers, expanded recycling education efforts, and packaging changes. SAB
Miller, the $25 billion brewing giant plans "to reduce by 25 percent the
amount of water used to brew each hectoliter of beer."[1] The company also
plans to reduce its fossil fuel usage and work toward well-defined sustainability goals. In fact, the company went through an internal audit and produced a sustainability report for the corporation worldwide.

SAB Miller is far from alone. In fact, the trend of businesses to move
toward sustainable practices and green initiatives is so widespread that
the real outliers are the companies that have yet to initiate such programs.
Electronic companies, such as Nokia, Samsung, and Sony Ericsson, have
been added to a Greenpeace list of the green electronic manufacturers
(although in the same report it was noted that some of the major computer manufacturers are behind in their green promises regarding the
manufacturing processes and materials used). Coca Cola announced that
one of their New York bottling facilities would get 30 percent of its power
from fuel-cell technologies. Sony Europe reported that, in 2008, through
the use of alternative energy and carbon offsets, they were at 100 percent
renewably produced energy.

Green business is here to stay, and it will be one of the fundamental cornerstones in a green collar economy. So far, the job sectors that have been discussed were based primarily in technical fields or are offshoots of traditional manufacturing and blue collar jobs. Over the next few chapters, we look at green job opportunities that are driven from the traditional white collar world of business, law, and marketing. It's in these fields that there is a marriage of real economic development sense and the desire to merge the fields of business and green. Businesses, after all, are an essential part of the green job promise. Most of the alternative energy jobs are in smaller private businesses. The jobs in green building use materials made by manufacturing companies, many of which got their start from working with venture capitalists. The list goes on, but the point is clear. Only by fully integrating business disciplines into the green economy can the promise of a green future truly work. As stated in Chapter 1, government can't do it all. It can offer the incentives and give some funding, but business leaders are going to be the ones who step up and transform the green economy into a larger segment of the country's output.

Green jobs are about creating economic opportunities, but also about "building entirely new businesses and upending markets."[2] In the Green Law chapter, we look at carbon trading, relating to limits on CO_2 production worldwide. But there are other areas where green business opportunities will arise. One of the most visible is as sustainability professionals and climate advisors to large multinational companies. These jobs bring the green world smack into the middle of the boardroom. By working with companies to comply with regulations, companies can reevaluate their internal processes not only to save expenses but also to use as a marketing angle. This relates to the next chapter, which concentrates on green marketing.

Green business degree programs are expanding at an exponential rate, fueled by the general increase in green collar job opportunities, coupled with students' awareness of sustainability issues and the real vision of a perfect marriage between environmental stewardship, social responsibility, and good business practices. The degree programs are designed to make students ready for the "reality of tomorrow's markets by equipping them with the social, environmental and economic perspectives required for business success in a competitive and fast changing world."[3]

Although it is technically a subset of green business, management of a mutual fund that invests in socially and environmentally responsible companies is a growing field. Mutual funds that look at green in the environmental sense, as well as in profits, are a "fast-growing corner of the fund universe that has seen a huge jump in interest in the last year or two."[4] More investors are taking a closer look at the sustainable practices of corporations. Likewise, capital firms and investment advisors that specialize in green companies are finding job opportunities, even among the ruins of the financial crisis of 2007–2009.

Green mutual funds and green financiers tend to back smaller upstart companies. These are some of the very companies that we profiled in previous chapters and identified as being the ones who will be the driving force behind the technical innovation needed to cope with the myriad of environmental issues that, in turn, drive green job growth. Because of the often volatile nature of start-ups, the rewards can be great, but so can the risks. Money managers working in these sectors need to manage risk well. Alternately, large corporations that are moving more into sustainability as a core of their business practice offer lower risk.

Green entrepreneur is a vague job descriptor that can really apply to about any green job around, but it is probably best housed with the green business category. Entrepreneurs can be water-resource managers, solar-power technicians, or green contractors. But the reason that this job is listed is because it may be currently the most important green job. The entrepreneurs who take the green ideas that are out there and turn them into a tangible product or service line and risk their investment to make it happen are the ones who will be giving out jobs as their businesses grow and the ones who will be at the technological forefront of the green job sector. Being an entrepreneur in green business takes little more than a solid background in business, good management skills, love of risk-taking, and money skill. A green entrepreneur also needs to understand green issues and not just throw a simple tag of green on a product.

The job outlook for green entrepreneurs is as high as for any other green career. The simple fact is that small businesses and entrepreneurship drive the U.S. economy to a large extent. So, in order for green careers to succeed, as noted earlier, there really needs to be a level of support from the private sector. As new technologies come out of research institutions and the government puts out more money to fund training programs for workers, the green entrepreneur will take those elements to the marketplace. And this ties back into the bigger picture of green business. The sustainable marketplace will only succeed if there is a willingness to take a chance on firms that believe in a green economy and look past the next quarter's performance to cultivate real long-term business models to emulate.

There is a tendency in the modern financial age to look at a company's health by its quarterly performance, not its long-term viability. Opponents of green jobs and anti-science activists are often quick to pounce on minor setbacks in the green economy or in new, allegedly green technologies (i.e., ethanol) that are not as environmentally sound as first thought. But that's the nature of an evolving business model. There needs to be a more firm commitment to see this through any short-term dips, whether fueled by general economic malaise or a real failure of a particular job sector or technological achievement. This is the only real way a green business system will work. Fortunately, there are many business professionals who see this and are working toward making that goal a reality.

Education and Job Resources/Organizations

The number of MBA programs with a concentration in sustainability or environmental issues is huge. To list all the schools would be a massive undertaking in and of itself. The following is a list of major organizations, educational resources, as well as job resources, to help people looking for degree programs in green business, internships and careers in green business, as well as getting the basic knowledge and background of some of the issues surrounding this relatively new segment of the business community, with some case studies and personal blogs from professionals in the field.

- Beyond Grey Pinstripes (www.beyondgreypinstripes.org). It's difficult to keep up with all the schools offering business programs with themes of environmental sustainability and outright green MBA programs. This Web site ranks the top 100 schools in the country for business programs with that sustainability and social progress concentration.
- Center for Sustainable Enterprise, University of North Carolina Kenan-Flagler (www.kenan-flagler.unc.edu/KI/cse/). The Center was established in 2001 and offers students a degree program with a concentration in Sustainable Enterprise. The program is interdisciplinary and focuses on a broad array of traditional business ventures tied in with the dual ideas of social and environmental sustainability.
- Corporations 4 Green (corporations4green.com/). This is a sustainable business consulting company. Although many of the larger corporations have these professionals in house, there are enough potential clients to make opening a consulting business a potentially profitable venture for the willing entrepreneur. The consultants work with companies to get a handle on their

carbon footprint and come up with cost-effective and marketable ways for them to reduce their environmental impact and come up with a plan to reduce costs and increase the bottom line. Corporations 4 Green is headquartered in Connecticut.

- EcoLife Consulting (ecolifeconsulting.com/). Another green business consulting company, Eco Life, based in California, advises companies on sustainability, works with green building, offers eco-consultant training programs, and does public outreach and education.
- Environmental Leader (www.environmentaleader.com). This site offers a daily briefing on issues relating to green business. Topics covered include leadership, strategy, finances, products, research and technology, and policy. The articles concentrate on private business ventures and real cost savings from sustainable business practices. The site also gives job seekers an idea of what companies are working with sustainability consultants, which ones have expanding programs, what private consulting companies are at the leading edge of green business, and where the green business opportunities are located.
- Green Biz (www.greenbiz.com). This site is a one-stop shop for green business news, resources, networking opportunities, and job openings. Green Biz also offers Greenbiz radio and Webcasts for additional outreach.
- Green Collar Economy (www.greencollareconomy.com/). This site is a business-to-business portal, designed along the lined of a LinkedIn, coupled with a general jobs board. The site has links to thousands of companies in all areas of green business and technology.
- Green Consulting Business Plan (www.greenconsulting businessplan.com/). I found this company at the top of a Google search page for green business ventures. They succeeded in Green Marketing 101. This is one of those customized courses to teach you how to enter the green business job market, how to be a consultant, where to get your clients, and how to familiarize yourself with green terms. For only $29.99 it might be a good deal, but I'm obviously not going to vouch for it. What this does say is that there are a lot of niche entrepreneurs who are looking for ways to capitalize on the green business model for their own benefit and, hopefully, the environment's as well.

- Green Inc. (greeninc.blogs.nytimes.com/). *The New York Times* blog devoted to "Energy, Environment, and the Bottom Line." The blog posts are often informative about trends in green business. There are links to various organizations and green job Web sites.
- Greentech Miami (mia-greentech.blogspot.com/). A green entrepreneur's blog on the possibilities and difficulties of green as a business venture. The blog is updated regularly, and it has a LinkedIn group to join.
- Green2Gold (www.green2gold.org). This is a nonprofit group that helps green businesses gain market share through education, marketing, mentoring, and business assistance. This organization is a good resource for any entrepreneurs looking to start up a sustainable service or product-based business.
- Net Impact (www.netimpact.org). Net Impact is a nonprofit group that comprises students, MBAs, and business professionals—with the goal of bringing a sense of sustainability and environmental awareness (as well as social progress) to the business community. It has a wide variety of programs, including a volunteer group that works with other nonprofits, a college student outreach program, and a career center for job seekers and prospective employees.
- Sustainable Business Design (http://sustainablebusiness design.blogspot.com/). This is a blog that examines the concept of sustainability as it relates to businesses. It lists an impressive number of related links, Web seminars, and education institutions that offer degrees in green business. One thing that really stands out on this blog is the range and quality of the articles and resources that are presented.

CHAPTER 7

GREEN MARKETING

The concept of green marketing is based on the premise that consumers want to feel like they are not only buying a high-quality product but one that either is good for the environment or was made with minimal impact to it. The idea of choosing to do the right thing is a powerful motivator, and, coupled with the ever-increasing awareness of environmental issues by the general public, the marketing sector dedicated to green marketing has been growing in recent years. As with the other career paths featured in this guide, green marketing is a fairly new track that is built on an established career. The American Marketing Association succinctly defines green marketing as "the marketing of products that are assumed to be environmentally safe."[1] Green marketing can also comprise "a variety of activities, including modifications to products, changes to the production and distribution processes, packaging changes, and modifications to marketing communications."[2]

Green marketing takes either new or established products and services and puts out the idea that these products are different in that they give or are conducive to a benefit that can be intangible—as intangible to the consumer as simply feeling like they did the right thing. But marketing green is also important for many of the new technologies and companies that are at the cutting edge of new breakthroughs in environmental technology. Without having the marketing know-how and background in science, marketers can do little to help these entrepreneurs when they need to sell their product to the public.

The rise in green marketing, more so than any of the other environmental careers, is based on awareness of environmental issues. In some
sense, public education and outreach efforts by environmental organizations, scientific bodies, and governments have been sort of a marketing
campaign to educate the public on the environment. Job opportunities
exist there, and we explore them later in this chapter. But consumer sen-
timent has spilled over into buying power. Consumers, says one journalist, "derive a sense of achievement from contributing to this cause and are
on the lookout for words like 'eco-friendly,' 'organic,' etc."[3] To this end,
says John Merlino, it's vital for companies that want to compete in the
global marketplace to "infuse green products, best practices, and marketing into their current business models."[4]

Capitalism may have its ups and downs, but it has been the dominant
force in the economic ascension of the United States. And although the
seemingly incongruity of business and environment may be on the wane
somewhat, there are businesses that still view the two subjects as unre-
lated. But that is where the consumer comes in. The choice made with the
wallet has the potential to have major effects on how businesses not only
offer products, but how those products are made, where they are made,
what type of perceived environmental benefit they have, and what the
perception of the company is as an environmental steward in regard to
its products. "Each time a product like a hybrid car or low-energy light
bulb gains a large market, it sends a message to CEOs, stock analysts,
institutional investors and venture capital funds."[5]

A better way to explain the benefits from green marketing for companies to improve their bottom line is simple. Company A can tout its
green advantage, "we're a company that supports green messages, operates using sustainable practices, greener packaging, etc. You should buy
from us because we are better stewards of the environment." It's a competitive edge in many marketplaces. You can see the changes in the food
aisles. Everything is becoming organic. And even though, as discussed
later in this chapter, the concept of organic has a nebulous definition, the
definite economic impact is a positive one for companies that use organic
products. The food costs more to make and to buy, but the feeling of
doing something right for the environment and for their health trumps
those considerations for consumers.

An early example of green marketing is the Energy Star program,
developed by the U.S. government in 1992. Whenever consumers purchase appliances, they can see the products' Energy Star rating letting
them know how energy-efficient the product is. Manufacturers concentrate their marketing efforts on product lines with favorable Energy Star

scores. The results have been excellent for companies that strive for the best Energy Star ratings. And recent reports have shown that households that use Energy Star-rated appliances do indeed save more on power bills than households that use less efficient appliances. Similar energy efficiency rating programs also exist in Europe.

Although green marketing to potential customers may be an uphill battle at times, the same can also be true for marketing internally within a company. One of the greatest challenges to green marketing within a company is the idea that going green will not only save money but bring additional benefits when marketing services to the public. Many companies feel forced to go green as a result of environmental regulations, and, as with anything that you are forced to do, especially under threat of a fine or legal enforcement, there is a potential for backlash. Because of the sometimes onerous regulations, many companies fail to get excited over the actual environmental benefit but rather view any environmental program in the company as a necessary evil to placate the regulators and, at least on the surface, make the half-hearted attempt to be an environmentally responsible company.

But there are companies that have whole-heartedly embraced the sustainability concept as not only the right thing to do, but because of the marketing impact. These are companies that seek to be simply socially responsible and use that drive for sustainability, to work together with the market and a well-executed marketing plan to enhance the company's profits. Other companies simply saw competitors taking the torch of sustainability and running with it, leaving them in the dust. Competition is a powerful motivator. If Company A sees that the business across the street is suddenly advertising that it is donating to local environmental charities and that it runs its store with power derived from alternative energy, Company A will likely follow suit. The public perception, whether correct or not, will be that the business across the street is doing the right thing and cares more about the environment than the bottom line. In reality, they care about both. There are a few naysayers who think that companies should concentrate on the bottom line solely, but, as the green movement has taken hold, ideological issues are often found to be compatible with monetary goals.

Most major international corporations now have offices of sustainability and green marketers on staff—not only to get the word out to the public about the advancements in going green that the companies are doing in-house, but also to parlay that into better sales and a stronger position in the marketplace. The driving force behind green marketing in many cases is money, both in revenue and expense savings. Bank of

America reduced paper consumption in its company by 32 percent between 2000 and 2005 and "recycles 30,000 tons of paper each year, good for saving roughly 200,000 trees for each year of the program's operation."[6]

The idea of sustainable food production is another segment of green marketing that has exploded in recent years, fueled by a few disparate lines. One is the concept of local marketing that is getting to consumers the information that the food they are buying is locally grown, caught, or produced, or at least was transported from a neighboring state or region. This also plays into the concept of buying non–genetically modified food and buying certain produce in season. To further break down the various subsets of this concept is beyond the scope of this guide, but suffice it to say the way that consumers think about food is changing dramatically, and marketers need to be up to speed on the latest developments and issues. Fast food titans such as McDonalds have gotten in on the act. Mickey D's works with People for the Ethical Treatment of Animals (PETA) "on systematically reforming its business practices to be more humane and friendly to the environment in which they operate."[7]

There is a potential pitfall and dark side to green marketing called *greenwashing*. Greenwashing is a term, coined by environmental activist Jaw Westerveld, used to call out the fake greens, the ones that use the veneer of sustainability to advance their business without really putting the effort behind it to be truly green. Westerveld came up with the term after looking at placards in hotels describing how reusing guest towels made the hotel somehow greener. This has become the accepted term for critically assessing the sustainability claims of companies that suddenly want to be green but really don't put much effort into it. Greenwashing companies are often outed on environmental blogs and magazines and taken to task publicly. Often the companies realize that fighting this is a public relations nightmare, and the easier track to take is actually to work toward being more sustainable and be able to defend their green claims.

Another ancillary green marketing job is environmental education. Public education and outreach are not really about marketing products, but more about selling a message. The concept of public education is an integral part of a lot of green jobs, especially those relating to environmental issues at a government level, whether state or local. Many government agencies have a media relations or outreach department that is equipped to deal with public inquiries and handle environmental complaints. Public outreach and education can be a part of environmental permits such as NPDES or as a condition for some grants. Many government agencies do outreach events such as conferences, workshops, community and civic group events, speaking engagements, and school events. The idea behind the increased outreach to the public is, first, to get people to understand particular ecological issues in plain language and to see the issue for themselves. Second, it's to market the idea of the government service or project to get their buy-in. Once people see what kind of benefit they'll derive from an ecological perspective, it knocks down a lot of barriers in communication.

The public can be a tough group to get up in front of and persuade. I know this from experience in trying to sell people the merits of a stormwater improvement project that the county I was working for was trying to get off the ground. The project was designed to help the status of the lake that they all lived on. People constantly complained about the lake's condition but were equally vocal in opposition to some of the proposed remedies. After a series of public meetings and public outreach events that our department did (native vegetation plantings, clean-ups), and a lot of simply being available to talk to the citizens, there was a palpable sense of a sea change in their feelings toward the project. That, in essence, was green marketing—for a message and, to some extent, a product. The product, in this case, was a project in which a lot of people invested a lot of time and money.

Speaking to kids can also be a tough gig, but a very rewarding one. Part of public outreach starts with educating the youngest citizens about green concepts and environmental ideas. With kids, the marketing aspect is almost nonexistent. It's far more a matter of just giving them the basics—don't litter, don't dump junk down the storm drain—or simple messages for them to take home. Speaking to school groups about potential green collar or general science careers is another way to market green ideas, but from a more practical perspective. This is especially good with career days. I recently spoke to high-schoolers at the academy where my wife teaches and described a variety of green jobs, the education needed, and the job outlooks. A few of the students asked some pointed questions and said that they were even more interested in some of the positions I spoke about. It's rewarding to be able to help students out in deciding how they want to go in their future career.

Social marketing studies based on public outreach ideas, especially dealing with environmental issues, are a growing trend among NGOs and government departments looking to monitor the effectiveness of marketing campaigns. For example, a recent social marketing study I was a part of looked at the attitudes of dog owners and of the general public about picking up after their animals as it related to the degradation in water quality of nearby water bodies. This study was effective in ascertaining how the respondents viewed various outreach efforts to educate the general public. Similar efforts are mirrored in nationwide programs, such as storm drain marking. Residents see storm drains marked with a plaque or stencil telling them not to dump debris into the drain—that the drain dumps directly into a nearby water body.

Where the Jobs Are

Most green marketing jobs are within existing companies, to bring ideas of sustainability and green ethos into their products, or within companies that offer marketing and branding services to public and private clients. A few companies that specialize in green marketing are featured later in this chapter, but there are not nearly as many small marketing firms specializing in green as other environmental sectors. This may be an opportunity to move into an area with less competition for an entrepreneurial-spirited business person with a knowledge of marketing.

Social marketing and public marketing jobs can be found in NGOs and government departments, especially environmental departments or agencies that deal with permit regulations and compliance. Many environmental permit programs require outreach and education as a prerequisite for the permit.

For decades, Manhattan was the epicenter of marketing. The fabled Mad Men of Madison Avenue were fairly close to reality. In recent years, although New York City still has a strong advertising presence, markets have emerged in smaller cities and in areas far outside the traditional strong holds. College towns, such as Madison, Wisconsin, and Boston, Massachusetts, are becoming hotbeds of innovation and entrepreneurial visions. In these cities and in smaller college towns, green marketing is becoming a more dominant player.

For internal company sustainability consulting and marketing, any city with a strong business community or one with a strong technology-driven populace would be a great place for job seekers. The traditional marketing havens of New York City and Chicago are still good choices, as are Los Angeles and San Francisco. But smaller college towns where a lot of the research-driven upstarts are located might be a wise move as well. You can find small niche marketing firms there, or go off on your own to form a marketing company that works with specific green careers or with companies that specialize in certain green products. Whatever you decide to, it would be worthwhile to research the specifics of the companies in the area you are looking to relocate to, before you make the jump.

Job Resources

- American Marketing Association (AMA) Job Board (www.marketing power.com/Careers/Pages/JobBoard.aspx). Although it is a general marketing job site, the AMA site is a comprehensive source for all marketing sectors, including green.
- The Business of Green (money.cnn.com/magazines/fortune/ greenbiz/). *Fortune* magazine has an excellent video-based site that looks at the edge of green marketing and entrepreneurship, showcasing companies that do everything from eco-remediation to recycling strategies to alternative energy. It's one of the most up-to-date and useful sites on green business.
- Enviral Marketing Blog (www.enviralmarketingblog.com). This is a blog that looks at the latest trends in environmental marketing. A little thin at the time of the book's writing, in mid-2009, the blog does have a green jobs board with marketing positions, mainly in the United States.
- Green Maven (www.greenmaven.com/green-marketing). This Web site is a general green directory, but it also features a section devoted to green marketing featuring job openings, primarily in the United States.
- Good and Green (www.goodandgreen.biz). Good and Green is a green marketing conference that was most recently held in November 2009 in Chicago. Check the Web site for future locations. Conferences are always an excellent place to network.
- Marketing Jobs.com (www.marketingjobs.com). One of the largest general sales and marketing jobsites on the Web, it has hundreds of green marketing jobs, generally found under the keyword "environmental."
- Marketing Crossing (www.marketingcrossing.com). This site charges a monthly fee, but it claims to be one of the premier repositories of marketing jobs, based in part on the fact that, unlike some of the larger commercial job sites, it does not charge employers to post their jobs on the site. The site also features marketing jobs from a variety of countries.
- Marketing Green (www.marketinggreen.wordpress.com). This is a blog devoted to green marketing and sustainable practices

in the field. Although it is infrequently updated, it has a wealth of information for those interested in green marketing.
- Only Marketing Jobs (www.onlymarketingjobs.com). This site features positions primarily in the United Kingdom, although it does also have marketing positions in other countries, including the United States. Another general marketing site, it also features environmental and green marketing positions.
- Sustainable Business (www.sustainablejobs.com). A general green job site, with a large section devoted to green sales and marketing jobs, as well as outreach and advocacy, which can encompass social marketing jobs. The jobs are not only in the United States, but in a variety of other countries from Europe to the Caribbean. Positions range from development directors, to sales managers, to trade show exhibitors, to entry-level associates.

Companies/Organizations

- American Marketing Association (www.marketingpower.com). The premier marketing professional organization in the United States, the American Marketing Association is at the forefront of green and sustainable marketing initiatives and ideas.
- Clear Green Radio (www.cleargreenradio.com). Do you have a product that you'd like to advertise on the radio? Is your green product needing a boost of marketing power? This company melds green marketing with mass media and outreach to get its clients choice ad spots on radio stations nationwide. It's a truly unique green niche company.
- Green Marketing Coalition (http://greenmarketingcoalition .com/). Founded in 2007, this marketing organization deals exclusively with green marketing concepts, including bringing ideas of sustainability to its clients for both environmental and economic benefits. The organization also has a list of green marketing guidelines and a regularly updated Web site with related articles.
- Green Marketing, Inc. (www.greenmarketing.net). Another well-known green marketing and communications firm, this Colorado-based company offers a wide variety of green services, including marketing consulting.
- ICLEI, Local Governments for Sustainability (www.icleiusa .org/action-center/financing-staffing/job-openings). This site has some good resources for people looking to work as sustain-

ability professionals and marketers for local governments. As noted in earlier chapters, working for public entities can be lower-paying, but it is often more stable, with good benefits.

- J. Ottoman Consulting (www.greenmarketing.com). Jacqueline Ottoman is one of the pioneers in green marketing. Her company is one of the most widely recognized in the field and regularly helps top Fortune 500 companies with their green marketing needs. The company Web site has a blog and articles about various topics in green marketing. A must-stop for anyone interested in the field.
- Productive Knowledge (www.productiveknowledge com/ greenmarketing.php). This company is a general marketing company, but it also specializes in green marketing and public relations. The company is based in Milwaukee, Wisconsin.
- Rocky Mountain Institute (www.rmi.org/). The Rocky Mountain Institute is a nonprofit company based in Colorado. It is one of the largest environmental advocacy groups for green business and sustainability in the nonprofit sector. It works with businesses in developing sustainable strategies for shaping the corporate image, reducing energy usage, and helping companies combine profit with economic growth. The group's unique vision is to merge the marketplace with the needs of the consumer, business, and environment. It is working to break down the barriers in perception between the various facets of green business.
- Sustainable Marketing (www.sustainablemarketing.com). This marketing company is so into sustainability that it offset 100 percent of its energy usage with wind power. It offers a broad range of marketing and sustainability consulting and computer services for public and private clients, ranging from Web design to graphic design, to marketing research. The site also has a membership area with discussion forums, blogs, reference library, and press releases.

CHAPTER 8

GREEN LAW

Just one week before finishing the first draft of this book, a colleague of mine came into the office after a recent meeting of the Tampa Bay Nitrogen Management Consortium. The group comprises representatives from state agencies, local governments, and private companies. The goal of the consortium is to address nitrogen loadings into Tampa Bay and, more recently, to come up with equitable nutrient allocations for each entity to satisfy a reasonable assurance plan for nitrogen TMDL compliance for Tampa Bay. I asked him how things were going. He said that they were going to get even more complicated than they had been. "The lawyers are coming to the table," he said, half-laughing. And he was right, the complex plan to allocate nutrient loads was coming toward its final stretch and the lawyers were moving into make sure that that their clients were protected properly, whether it was the implementation of the plan or the compliance with the plan or how the Florida Department of Environmental Protection was going to turn the load requirements into permits.

The lawyers had backgrounds in environmental issues; some were even former scientists. The field of environmental law is centered on the interpretation of laws relating to environmental stewardship and human usage of natural resources. Environmental regulations are growing, complexity is increasing, and environmental law is booming. Law schools, like Lewis and Clark Law School, are expanding their environmental departments and seeing enrollment skyrocket. For those going into law school or thinking about a field in law, environmental services may prove to be a viable and exciting career path. Environmental law is far from a new concept. It's one of the cornerstones of the modern legal profession. More often than not, the image of an environmental lawyer is as a representative of an NGO, suing the government for not enforcing existing environmental laws, or of a law office going after a major polluter, the kind seen in Hollywood movies such as *A Civil Action* and *Erin Brockovich*. In fact, many lawyers are representing groups as diverse as recreational fishermen, coal companies, local governments, and citizens.

It's estimated that, although there are over 15,000 environmental lawyers currently in the United States, jobs are expected to grow by "18 to 25 percent over the next decade."[1] Environmental lawyers are on retainer for everything from large corporations to citizens' groups. The lawyers offer a wall of protection for companies dealing with regulatory agencies and compliance with the often myriad of environmental permits and requirements from federal, state, tribal, and local governments. The lawyers are often on the front edge of changes in regulations and standards and work closely with the regulatory agencies to craft responsible, sensible bills. Most environmental lawyers I have had dealings with were extremely knowledgeable about the science and pragmatic in dealing with their clients. These days, it behooves a company to be as environmentally compliant as possible—not only from the perspective that failing to meet environmental requirements can result in fines and bad press, but being a responsible steward is a public relations boon and, in fact, necessary for a successful business plan.

Activist organizations and NGOs often use environmental lawyers to assist in their suits against governments and private companies. The group Earthjustice's tagline is "because the earth needs a good lawyer." The group works with everything from community groups to large coalitions and represents them in suits dealing with regulatory changes, endangered species, pollution cases, and reparations for environmental disasters. Many of the group's cases are taken *pro bono*, because the group is a nonprofit enterprise. The group also lobbies in Washington to strengthen environmental laws. Environmental activist organizations are responsible for many of the regulatory changes and frameworks that current environmental law is built around. Environmental lawyers spearheaded legal challenges to the Clean Water Act, which got the EPA to kick-start the TMDL program in states like Florida. Florida is currently feeling the effects of another activist suit that is pushing forward numeric nutrient criteria for water bodies throughout the state. Although needed, if only to bring some specificity to the all-too-vague rules in place, the criteria may not have gotten started at all had it not been for the lawsuit.

The interesting part about environmental law is that the activist lawyers are sometimes on the other side of the table from the firms representing corporations, especially in high-profile pollution suits or cases that have a good chance of having a major effect on current case law. It's easy to pick the side of the environmental activists from a purely green standpoint, but that's not always the situation. Each case is different, and people looking to get into environmental law can choose either side of the aisle and be comfortable that they are doing their part for the environment.

Environmental lawyers can specialize in a certain area, such as water-resources or endangered-species law. One of the most complex current legal environmental issues is the cap-and-trade program relating to global climate change. The idea is simple in concept. An industry gets a cap on the amount of carbon dioxide it can emit. This cap is enforced through a permit, much like a waste or stormwater permit. Some companies may have a hard time reaching their reduction goals; others can do it more effectively. Those companies that can reach their reduction may sell their additional permits (effectively credits) to the other companies. The implications from an economic perspective are apparent. As carbon trading grows in acceptance, "the market could grow to $500 billion by 2050."[2]

Cap-and-trade can be a business opportunity for companies that can sell their excess reductions and for middle-level entrepreneurs who view selling the permits on the open market as no different from selling products through a store. But it is going to be an area where companies that are affected by these regulations are going to need keen lawyers who can work their way through the maze of regulation and ensure that their clients are not only following the law, but doing what they need to stay a viable and profitable business. The cap-and-trade program has been praised and assailed, but the truth of how effective it will be or how detrimental to business it will end up is probably somewhere in the middle between these two extremes. And a good environmental lawyer, with a clear idea of the issue, can make all the difference.

Education

Many law schools have added environmental law majors to their curriculum. The following is a brief list of some of the more well-known environmental law programs.

- Golden Gate University School of Law (various locations). (www.law.umaryland.edu/environment/)—Golden Gate's environmental law program is another highly ranked program. The university features the Environmental Law & Justice Clinic, where students can get practical training experience in environmental law. The school publishes the *Environmental Law Journal* as well.

- Pace University School of Law, White Plains, New York (www.law.pace.edu/). Pace's environmental law department is among the top-ranked programs in the country. The program concentrates on general environmental law, with concentrations in climate change, pollution control and regulations, land use, and energy. The school publishes the *Green Law Journal* and hosts a variety of symposiums and conferences throughout the year. Pace is also partnered with the International Union for the Conservation of Nature.
- Stanford University Environmental and Natural Resources Law and Policy Program (www.law.stanford.edu/program/ centers/ enrlp/). One of the smaller law schools in the country, the Stanford environmental law program is nonetheless highly respected in the field. Students are involved in hands-on case work, programs with the Environmental Law Clinic, and working on the *Stanford Environmental Law Journal.*
- Stetson University College of Law, Gulfport, Florida (justice.law.stetson.edu/environmental/). Stetson University's Institute for Biodiversity Law and Policy is an education and research arm of the school of law. Courses reach into more ecological topics than some other law schools, and the focus on biodiversity is a unique curriculum focal point. The college also hosts conferences and the International Environmental Moot Court Competition.
- University of Maryland, Environmental Law (www.law .umaryland.edu/environment/). The environmental law department at Maryland is another well-regarded program that combines instruction with hands-on case studies. The school also publishes a biannual newsletter, *Environmental Law in Maryland.*
- Vermont Law School, Environmental Law Center (ELC) (www.vermontlaw.edu/). The ELC at the Vermont Law School is regularly ranked as one of the best environmental law programs in the country. It also boasts the largest graduating class of any environmental law program. The Center offers over 50 courses in a variety of ecological and law topics, as well as giving

students the chance for hands-on learning while working real cases. The institutes on campus include the Institute for Energy and the Environment, Environmental Tax Policy Institute, Climate Legacy Institute, Land Use Institute, and the unique Partnership for Environmental Law in China, which works on developing environmental laws and regulations in China.

- Lewis and Clark, Environmental and Natural Resources Law-Oregon (law.lclark.edu/programs/environmental_and _natural_resources_law/clinics_and_institutes.php). The Lewis and Clark law program concentrates on natural resources and animal law. The Pacific Environmental Advocacy Center, an environmental activist group working on ecological problems in the Pacific Northwest, is located on the school's campus and works closely with the environmental law program and allows students hands-on work with actual cases, from inception through work on the actual cases. It's designed to give the law students a heads-up for future work opportunities upon graduation. The school is also home to the Center for Animal Law Studies, a think tank on animal law issues and cases that also works with students for hands-on experience. Two other institutions on campus are the International Environmental Law Project and the Natural Resources Law Institute.

- University of California, Berkeley (Boalt Hall School of Law) (www.law.berkeley.edu/). Berkeley has one of the older environmental law programs in the country. It publishes the *Ecology Law Quarterly*, one of the leading environmental law journals. Students conduct hands-on local environmental projects in addition to coursework on general environmental law topics.

- University of Utah S. J. Quinney College of Law (www.law.utah .edu/stegner/degree-programs/). The University of Utah offers degrees in environmental and natural resources law. Courses include water law, Indian law, wildlife protection, and international environmental issues.

Job Resources

The main places to look for environmental law positions are the same places as for general lawyer positions. Many large firms have teams of environmental lawyers, and there are also small, niche firms that specialize in environmental law, water resources, natural resources, and endangered species. It's important to do some digging about the firms and what types of law they practice and who their clients are. Another way to get a feel for where the good environmental jobs are or where the need might be in the future is to track where some major upcoming environmental regulations are brewing. By getting a sense of where the next fights over laws will be, it's a good bet that there will be a need for well-qualified environmental lawyers. The following are law organizations, nonprofit law firms, and advocacy groups that can get job seekers started looking for that right environmental law career.

- Earthjustice (www.earthjustice.org). Previously profiled, this is one of the larger nonprofit law firms dedicated to environmental work. It is currently working on cap-and-trade and climate change issues.
- Environmental Law and Policy Center (elpc.org/category/jobs). The Center is headquartered in Chicago, with offices across the Midwest. It works almost exclusively on environmental issues in the Midwest. The job openings range from attorney to legislative liaisons and public interest specialists.
- Environmental Law Institute (www.eli.org). The Environmental Law Institute provides leadership in environmental law and policy. It was founded 40 years ago and is the premier law association for environmental policy. The Institute publishes numerous law books, reports, journals, and newsletters.
- Great Rivers Environmental Law Center (www.greatriverslaw .org). A nonprofit environmental law firm based in Missouri, the Center specializes in natural resource issues relating to the Missouri and Mississippi Rivers.
- Green Building Law Blog (www.greenbuildinglawblog.com/). Attorney Shari Shapiro's blog is an in-depth look at a variety of legal issues relating to green building, sustainability, climate change, and regulations relating to all the previous topics. The blog's entries clearly explain some of the more arcane pieces of legislation coming down the pike; it's also not afraid to make critical assessments of environmental policies.
- National Resources Defense Council (NRDC) (www.nrdec.org). The NRDC is another environmental activist organization with a strong environmental law component. Sometimes controversial, the NRDC works on a lot of endangered species and climate change issues.
- Southern Environmental Law Center (www.southernenvironment .org). It's the only organization specifically dedicated to working

on natural resource issues in the Southeast. The Center works
closely with regional governments as well as efforts in
Washington DC.

- WildLaw (www.wildlaw.org). A small firm, with offices in
  Florida, Alabama, and North Carolina, that specializes in
  national forest issues, as well as water quality and endangered
  species.

CHAPTER 9

THE GREEN WORLD

Although this book has focused primarily on green jobs in the United States, one fact of modern business is that there is indeed a global marketplace and a global village when it comes to business. And because environmental issues are not relegated to the United States alone, the opportunities for green jobs are indeed worldwide. With English being spoken in most parts of the globe, there are options for job seekers with limited foreign language skills. Also, although environmental issues are at the core local in nature, there are some green jobs that can transcend geographical differences. Solar and wind power technicians will find products overseas that are similar to what they find in the United States, for example. It's not always easy to get a job in a foreign country, but this chapter has some sources for potential employment if you choose to go the world traveler or expatriate route.

But knowing about green issues worldwide and having a finger on the pulse of the international environmental community might be equally as important for green collar workers in the United States. The global marketplace has made travel and dealings with foreign companies a lot more common now than it was 20 years ago. Green workers in the United States may have to deal with counterparts across the globe, working on global solution to environmental issues, working on alternative energy designs, discussing green building projects that a major U.S. company might be doing in Europe or that a Spanish company is doing in the United States, and working on global marketing strategies for the latest product. College graduates won't just be looking for jobs in their college town or back home near Mom and Dad. The opportunities for work across the globe are far more accessible now than ever before and will only increase as more countries rise from poverty and enter the market.

Uniting the world in a green economy won't be particularly easy. For one, there are geopolitical issues that exist, and being an American in some parts of the world is not always the safest. There are economic concerns, especially as a result of the economic disparity that exists throughout much of the globe. Third World countries are more worried about how they are going to feed their population or how their citizens can earn a living wage working on an oil rig than worrying about climate change or other abstract environmental issues. The catch-22, of course, is that they are going to be the ones most affected by changes in weather patterns and the economic turmoil that further environmental damage will bring to their region. This is especially true in parts of Africa and Asia, where poverty and environmental destruction go hand in hand, renewing the cycle and turning the whole situation into a continuous downward spiral. Even here in the Western Hemisphere, impoverished Central American countries will have a harder time implementing green job training programs that more affluent ones in North and South America.

But for job possibilities in green collar careers, the first place someone looking for international experience should investigate is Europe. Western Europe has been at the forefront of green jobs for longer than the United States. Countries such as Germany, Spain, Norway, Finland, Sweden, and Denmark have been exploring alternative energy seriously for decades. France has turned to nuclear energy to provide much of the country's electricity. A recent report by the World Wildlife Institute reported that over 3.4 million jobs in Europe are "directly related to renewable energy, sustainable transport and energy-efficient goods and services."[1] Indirect jobs relating to these green careers are estimated to be over 5 million. At the leading edge of clean energy are Germany and Denmark for wind and Germany and Spain for solar. Green technologies are the subject of heavy investment by the government, and training programs are often fully paid for. It's easy to wish that for the United States, but it also needs to be stated that European countries work on a different economic model than the United States.

Even in Europe, there are wide disparities. Even though the Western European countries are firmly ahead in the green collar economy, large swaths of Eastern Europe, especially the former Soviet bloc countries, are still lagging behind. Some are buoyed up by natural gas and oil reserves; others are still into dirty manufacturing practices and paying the ecological price. Still, some other countries are closing the gap, as clean energy policies adopted by the European Union work their way into the economies of the member countries. Russia is an example of a country where the green revolution is getting underway, but, because of the vast and plentiful natural oil and coal resources, it won't be as attractive, at least in the short term.

The Middle East, being the epicenter of the world's oil, would hardly be a place where you would expect any kind of passion for green jobs. "The Middle East and the UAE, in particular, are the world's most inefficient energy users in terms of per capita oil usage."[2] But many of the governments there realize that they will eventually have to deal with climate change issues, as well as with their best customers in the West weaning themselves from their product. The one advantage of some of the oil-producing countries in the region is an excess of capital. That is particularly true in Dubai, Qatar, and Saudi Arabia. At the 2008 WEFTEC conference in Chicago, Dubai had a booth with examples of all the cutting-edge work people there are doing in desalination, geological engineering, energy conservation, and air pollution reduction. The government has money to spend and is not unaware of the global and regional environmental issues. Some Middle Eastern countries are getting in on solar and wind projects; others are setting up global sustainability funds to bankroll cap-and-trade programs and clean technology. All of this shows that the Middle East "is starting to seriously think about their own strategy for a world with far less dependence on oil."[3]

Australia is coping with a need to ensure a constant energy source for the future as its population grows. The government has been funding various renewable energy programs for the past decade. Most recently, the government Department of Resource, Energy and Tourism started the Renewable Energy Fund to "provide $500 million for a series of competitive grant programs that aim to demonstrate the viability of renewable energy technologies on a technical and economic basis."[4] It's hoped that this funding program will spur private investment into the technologies and create more green jobs.

One region that is in desperate need of economic development is Africa. For a country that is so associated with unspoiled savannahs, safaris, roaming herds of wildebeests, and some of the most unique habitats in the world, the continent has been a victim of despotic regimes, massive outbreaks of diseases, corruption, civil war, ethnic strife, and about every other problem you can come up with, all leading to an under-developed economy. The promise of renewable energy is beginning to take hold, even though some areas of the continent are rich in oil deposits. Jobs are being created, mainly by foreign firms looking to invest in developing markets as well as by African-based companies. Kestrel Wind Turbines is one of those firms. It's based in South Africa and has a worldwide presence. South Africa is also the place where innovative pro-grams using local youths to make shanty houses more energy-efficient and green have been taking hold. These programs combine the best elements of green job training with utilizing local employees and materials to work within their communities to improve the living condi-tions for their neighbors. Alternative ways to produce electricity will be the driving force for new innovation in Africa. Many of the remote villages do not have electricity. Companies are finding newer and cheaper ways to bring power to these places and improve the quality of life for the citizens.

Another green sector that has been expanding in Africa is organic farming. Most sustenance farming in Africa is by its nature organic. But many of the farmers are in poverty, barely able to feed their families, let alone work as suppliers to groceries. In South Africa, a pilot program worked with farmers in poverty-stricken villages to improve their farm-ing techniques. As a result, the farmers became a "major supplier of organic foods to one of South Africa's most prominent large retailers, Woolworths Holdings."[5] Similar efforts are working in other areas not only of sub- Saharan Africa but the North as well.

South America has been working toward greater usage of renewable resources. In Brazil, for instance, "45 percent of its energy comes from renewable sources."[6] South America has a geographical profile that would be ideal for solar and wind energy as well as hydroelectric power. In fact, a large portion of Brazil's alternative energy portion is derived from hydroelectric power. Other countries have not had as much success, although Argentina and Peru are hot spots for eco-tourism operations, as is Ecuador with its proximity to the Galápagos Islands.

Asian countries are split in their quest for green jobs. China is just getting on board the green collar economy, even as new coal-fired power plants open at an astounding rate. The country is trying to enhance the allure of its environmental ethos, but it's so far been drowned out by the relentless march to be the manufacturing hub of the world. As the population increasingly moves from the isolated rural areas to the cities and urbanization increases (with all the resultant ecological ramifications), China now sees itself caught in the cross-roads. It has recently made some efforts to spur green jobs creation and address ecological issues, especially in regard to air quality (as discussed in Chapter 5) and water-resource pollution. Other Asian countries, with the exception of North Korea, are already working hard on starting their green economic engines. Japan recently announced government plans to "expand the 'green business' market and create up to 1 million new jobs, with measures including zero-interest rate loans for environmentally-friendly companies. South Korea, meanwhile, will invest 38 billion dollars over the next four years in a series of eco-friendly projects to create 960,000 new jobs and lay the groundwork for economic growth."[7]

The outlook for work in foreign countries is up in the air, dependent on the economic conditions and potential political stability. Europe and Asia are safe bets for professionals interested in expanding their green job search. Some U.S.-based green jobs also have strong international components and can entail extensive travel. These jobs can range from green business consulting to environmental consulting and permitting. Many sustainable consultants who work for major corporations are tasked with taking the message of energy efficiency and sustainable practices to their foreign offices. In the next chapter, ecotourism is discussed. That is a career track that has a major overseas component to it.

Of course, working in a foreign country brings a host of issues—from language to cultural barriers to simple paperwork needed for getting the position. One easy way to get the lay of the land is to contact the nation's embassy in the United States. The embassy can be helpful in going over residency and visitor requirements for work permits. It can also expedite any processes that you may need to go through to work in the country. Again, those are areas that need to be researched when you are setting out to find opportunities in other countries. I once asked an Australian fisheries biologist about work he was doing in a marine lab on the Great Barrier Reef. It sounded so appealing, and I knew enough Australian fish names, even the scientific ones, to make it through the conversation with him. But when he told me about the residency requirements and difficulty in getting a job as a foreigner, it was a little reality check. That was back in 1996, so things may have changed. I know some colleagues who studied there and another who worked there for a while in a scientific lab.

Job Resources

Many of the job boards identified in previous chapters have international components, as do most of the major job search engines. The following sites are specifically tailored to certain geographical regions or job categories.

- BusinessGreen (www.businessgreen.com). This is a U.K.-based green business site that offers an assortment of videos, news items, publications, and a job board relating to green energy and business in the United Kingdom.
- Centre for Alternative Technology (www.cat.org.uk/jobs/). Based in Wales, this site offers job positions across Europe in sustainability and alternative technology. The Centre also hosts various training courses and seminars, offers consulting services to companies and governments, and publishes reports relating to renewable energy in Europe.
- China Green Buildings (chinagreenbuildings.blogspot.com/). This is an English-language blog on issues relating to green building and sustainability in China. It's a good place to get on-the-ground information about career opportunities and general green building trends.
- Edie (www.edie.net). This is an excellent general green resource Web site, with a large section of European green job opportunities. The Web site is based in the United Kingdom, so the jobs are concentrated there, but there are listing across continental Europe as well.
- Environmental Careers (www.environmentalcareers.org.uk/). Another general environmental career Web site based in the United Kingdom, it also lists upcoming conferences and seminars regarding various green topics.
- Environmental Data Services (ENDS) (www.ends.co.uk/). A European environmental news source, the ENDS Web site also has a job board.
- Environmental Jobs UK (www.environmentjob.co.uk/). With sectors ranging from organic farming to renewable energy to sustainable transport, this Web site offers the best source for green jobs in the United Kingdom. It's also useful for employers looking to advertise available positions.
- India Environmental Portal (www.indiaenvironmentportal .org.in/). This is a complex, in-depth Web site, with information

on the latest environmental issues in India in dozens of areas from green energy to biotech crops. The site offers a wealth of resources, including a section called "in-depth" with, as promised, in-depth reports on major environmental challenges in the subcontinent.

- Misco Jobs (www.miscojobs.com/). This site lists jobs in mining, fossil fuels, alternative energy, construction, and environmental sciences. Jobs are worldwide in scope. A site visitor can also post résumés on the job board.
- NRM Jobs (www.nrmjobs.com.au/). This Web site advertises hundreds of air, water, and general environmental jobs in Australasia. It also lists available academic positions, grants, and scholarships in the related fields.
- Oxford HR (www.oxfordhr.co.uk/). Oxford HR is a consulting agency specializing in bringing together qualified applicants to companies, NGOs, and governments working on international development, especially in Third World locations. There are a lot of positions in sustainable development and environmental activism as well as general environmental science.
- R-Energy (www.r-energy.info/en/). This site lists renewable energy expos held in various cities around the globe. The first three expos were held in Sao Paolo, Buenos Aires, and Istanbul.
- Riley Guide (www.rileyguide.com/americas.html). This is a good general career site for various international regions.
- Stop Dodo (www.stopdodo.com), Touted as the "global portal for environmental jobs & resumes," this site lives up to its promise. Visitors can choose from a dozen languages and find jobs in dozens of disciplines around the globe.
- Sustainable Energy in Africa (sustainableenergyinafrica .ning.com/). A general information blog about renewable energy in Africa, this is a good place to start to get a feel for the industry.
- United Nations Environment Programme Green Jobs Report (www.unep.org/labour_environment/features/greenjobs -report.asp). The United Nations released this report, a comprehensive assessment of sustainability and green job creation across the globe, with particular emphasis on Third World countries and what type of sustainable jobs will assist in economic development in those regions. The report also outlines prospects for various green job sectors.

- World Energy Source (www.worldenergysource.com/). The World Energy Source publishes the *World Energy Magazine*, broadcasts WorldEnergyTV, and has an active community of professionals in the energy field, from traditional oil and gas to renewables and alternative energy. The magazine regularly runs pieces from major energy corporations. There is also a comprehensive global job board on the Web site.

CHAPTER 10

MORE GREEN JOBS

The previous chapters discussed the major green job sectors, the alternative energy, the green law, and the businesspeople promoting sustainability. But there are more available careers to job seekers and probably many more that have yet to be created. The job market is opening up to all types of new hybrids between traditional jobs and their newer, greener counterparts. There are green versions of jobs in all areas, from design to sales. There are green jobs in electrical household product manufacturing, computer manufacturing, computer software design, landscaping, and academia. How this will all play out in the future is, of course, up in the air, but all the following green careers have good job outlooks—based on data from the U.S. Bureau of Labor Statistics, various commissioned reports on green jobs, anecdotal evidence from people in the field, and trends in the professional environmental community.

Green Journalism

In 2007, *Slate* magazine caused a minor stir in the environmental journalism community with the article "Green is the New Yellow," comparing the new green journalism to the populism and demagoguery of yellow journalism. The author made some insightful points about objectivity versus playing to an agenda-driven bias. He stated that green journalism "tends to appeal to our emotions, exploit our fears, and pander to our vanity."[1] His examples, taken in the context of the article, seemed more in line with paid advertisements for green products than serious stories. By outlining how far over the edge some journalists had fallen, the author also made a good case for why green/environmental journalism is an increasingly important and visible part of the journalism landscape.

Green journalism has a long pedigree as a subset of journalism. There have been journalists who specialize in environmental issues for local papers and national magazines, as well as niche journalists who covered regulations and goings-on in the government. It has traditionally been the arena of investigative journalists who had that aforementioned yellow journalism streak in them, digging into controversial environmental issues and running multi-day stories. Many careers were made on exposing environmental injustices, especially if they happened to be connected to powerful politicians or their friends in industry.

Other writers, such as outdoors section writers, especially in fishing and hunting, have often championed conservation causes through the written word. Some of the country's largest conservation organizations were formed or are backed by fishermen and hunters. That's a direct result of the advocacy journalism found in the pages of some papers' outdoors sections, as well as in magazines such as *Field and Stream* and *Florida Sportsman*. In fact, the *Florida Sportsman* exposed some environmental issues relating to fish and fish habitat that no other media source in Florida had uncovered and worked with conservation groups, such as the Coastal Conservation Association, to advocate rule changes for fish bag limits and habitat protection. That kind of writing falls squarely into the category of activism writing that some environmental journalists say is an important part of the field. As the *Slate* article pointed out, there can be that fine line between objectivity and bias, but some green journalists don't see that barrier as being an issue. They see the job of a green journalist as being the voice for the citizens in pushing for change and action. There are many, however, who see it as no different from any other type of journalism in terms of objectivity.

It's the environmental journalist's responsibility to take those often complex scientific and environmental issues and make them available and consumable by the general public. This can bring out the best in writing, or it can get overly confusing. Good environmental journalism spans the two worlds of science and writing and brings together a full-spectrum view of the issues. There have been some well-received and thought-provoking investigative journalism pieces in the last couple years. There was an investigative series by the *St. Petersburg Times* on wetland rules and regulations in Florida and how developers paved over 84,000 acres of wetlands without anyone having a clear idea of the amount that had been done. The pieces got so much attention that the two authors wrote a successful book on the subject. More recently, there was a *GQ* article, hardly a place you'd expect to find hard-hitting green reporting, on a massive coal ash spill that engulfed a Tennessee town, the myth of clean coal, and the fight by the town's residents to get their lives back. Both of these examples are illustrative of how the best environmental writing makes the issues accessible without getting preachy. The previously referenced *Slate* article outlines exactly what not to do.

Print journalism is an increasingly fading path. With newspapers in many parts of the country on their death knells, more journalism is taking place online. From purely online newspapers like *The Huffington Post* to magazines like *Slate*, journalists are increasingly disjointed from the Hollywood images of the giant bustling newsroom. And with the blogosphere becoming equally important as a source of information, having good green journalists to keep up with the latest technological, regulatory, and economic updates on the green front is increasingly essential. The word may not get out there as easily or in as concentrated a readership as the daily newspaper or a newsstand magazine, but the Web, for all its misinformation and just plain garbage, has become an important tool for journalists and writers to get their work out there to a large audience.

Like all good journalism, green reporters have to possess basic proficiency in writing, coupled with knowledge of science. It's a poorly kept secret that scientists are not always the best writers, in the sense that, although they can churn out a journal paper explaining the minutiae of narrowly focused scientific principles, they often have difficulty explaining the position to laymen. Science reporting has always filled that void. But with the intersection of science, technology, the environment, and green jobs, journalists now have to be well-versed in the terms, players, and topics. Familiarity with the complex world of environmental laws and regulations is also a sought-after skill. For the environmental journalist to be successful, he or she has to be flexible. Writing about change in nutrient criteria for springs one day and the ramifications of cap-and-trade on power plants the next day makes for a more employable writer than one who sticks to a specific niche topic. However, there are certain subgenres in environmental journalism. Some writers tend to stick to strictly scientific topics; others veer more toward science policy and law. Regardless, it's still best to be as amenable to different topics as possible.

One way for green journalists to get known in the field or to hone their writing craft is to start a green blog. Blogs are ubiquitous nowadays, but green blogs are still not as numerous as other topics, so there's a better chance for a budding environmental journalist to become known in the field. A comprehensive blog can take a little work at first, but it is worth it when the traffic starts flowing in. There are also many bloggers who make some money from the site through advertising or selling products directly. Selling products becomes a touchy topic and one that bloggers should ask their journalism ethics professors about to get a final ruling. But an environmental blog gives the chance to open your writing up to criticism and an audience. It's a cheap and easy way to get published, with a far greater chance of readership. Blogging is also a great networking tool. Comments sections can offer great tips on job opportunities, as well as making contacts in the professional and academic world.

One avenue that is sort of similar to journalism in that it takes a lot of great writing ability is a position as a grant writer. It's the job of a grant writer to get funding for municipal governments to fund their infrastructure and environmental projects. Grant writers are also essential for NGOs, academia, and start-up companies looking for alternative capital. As a grant writer, the professional must be fluent in basic scientific concepts as well as being up-to-date on state and federal levels with the funding opportunities that are available, the types of applications and information needed by the grantor agency, and the various deadlines for grant proposals. Grant writers need to have a firm handle on legislative matters and be able to communicate effectively with their employers or, if they are working for a consulting company, their clients. As fiscal resources and tax revenues decline, grant writer positions are hot commodities. But even during boom cycles of income to government coffers, grant writers are rarely without a grant application before them. Even though working the political system can have its advantages (lobbying is a case in point), it's more important to be knowledgeable about the process rather than the players. The job outlook for grant writers, especially ones who get results, is always solid.

Education Resources

- Knight Center for Environmental Journalism at Michigan State University (ej.msu.edu/about). Part of the School of Journalism, the Knight Center trains both students and working journalists in the finer aspects of covering environmental issues. The school publishes a green news magazine, as well as housing a collection of top environmental journalism articles. The school is also the home for the Environmental Journalism Association, the only student-led environmental news group in the country. The Center offers bachelor's and master's degrees in journalism, with a concentration in environmental journalism.

- Lehigh University (cas.lehigh.edu/). One of the older environmental journalism programs, established in 1978, Lehigh offers an undergraduate degree in science writing.
- Middlebury College (www.middlebury.edu). Middlebury College offers a fellowship in environmental journalists. Each year it takes 10 applicants through a comprehensive and rigorous reporting project. The competition is, understandably, tough for admission to the program.
- University of Colorado at Boulder (www.colorado.edu/journalism/cej/). Part of the School of Journalism and Mass Communication, the Center for Environmental Journalism at the university offers an MS program in environmental journalism. The Center works closely with a wide array of professional scientific organizations in the Boulder area.
- University of Missouri (www.journalism.missouri.edu). The Missouri School of Journalism offers a 2-year MA degree in environmental reporting.

Job Outlook/Resources

The future of environmental journalism is up in the air. In early 2009, BBC closed down its BBC Green Web site, and other news outlets scaled back their green writing departments. Blogs and specialty Web sites took up some of the slack, but there is a palpable sense by veteran environmental writers that it's not going to get easier for people looking to enter the field. Part of that, of course, has to do with the state of journalism itself, given a serious body blow by the ever-shrinking staffs at local newspapers. The recession of 2007–2009 went further, gutting many major news outlets and leading to the closing of scores of papers across the country. Some of the writers went online, where the pay is often lower, sometimes nonexistent. Although the promise of writing careers on the Web has been made, these promises often are not as they appear, especially when it comes to salary.

- CE Journal (www.cejournal.net/). A blog-heavy Web site from the University of Colorado, it focuses exclusively on environmental journalism.

- Journalism Jobs (www.journalismjobs.com/). This is a general journalism job site with information on environmental journalism openings.
- Society of Environmental Journalists (www.sej.org/). Like any other field, it's essential to get involved with an organization of like-minded professionals. For environmental/green journalists, the Society of Environmental Journalists is a good choice. The Society also has an interesting library section with books, blogs, industry trend reports, and links to freelance journalism sites.

Ecotourism

Green tourism, alternately known as ecotourism, is increasing at a rapid rate and is becoming a greater percentage of the tourism sector itself. Ecotrips are now offered throughout the United States, in addition to the traditional ecotourist spots, like the Galápagos Islands. Ecotourism has been touted as a way to spur economic development in poorer regions of the world and has been, for the most part, embraced by the environmental community. Ecotourism is more than hiking up a mountain to look at scenery. It's interacting with local indigenous people, it's gaining an appreciation for the natural world and the role sustainability has in preserving it, and it's a great job for people who love to be outdoors, love to teach others, have an entrepreneurial zeal, and who have a deep affection for the road less traveled.

Ecotourism jobs can be varied, although they fall mainly along the lines of company operators, tour guides, and owners of residences (hotels, huts, etc.). Many ecotourism jobs are with private companies, but there are a number of government jobs at local parks and preserves, state forests, and national monuments. There can be a variety of positions or the job can limited to taking groups up the same slope or talking about the same animals over and over. It really depends on the unique employment situation.

Employment is seasonal. Tour guides work mainly during the tourist seasons. In the United States, most tour operators close up for the winter. However, there are some that specialize in winter tours. It depends. Working in a green hotel or lodging facilities associated with ecotourism can be a year-round position. Also some parks and preserves have full-time staff year-round to carry out routine maintenance as well as research.

Public outreach is an essential aspect of most ecotourism jobs. The tours are supposed to educate the customers on wildlife ecology and customs of the local area. So, even if you travel to a different country to work for a tour group, you need to become an expert overnight in the flora and fauna of your new job location. Also, making sure you are comfortable speaking to groups, both large and small, is probably a good idea before you're put in front of a crowd of tourists explaining the difference between two snakes you see slithering across the hiking trail.

The popular conception of ecotourism is a remote lodge in a far-away country that takes days to get to after hiking through a rain forest. In fact, there are thousands of places in the United States to go for short day trips, to stay and hike for a long weekend, or to stay for a season. Ecotourism has merged with traditional and newer outdoor sports, such as hiking and kayaking. Even fishing guides now offer ecological tours. In Florida the flats offer a bounty of game fish for anglers, but also excellent birding, snorkeling, and watching marine life. Ecotourism at a local level is more popular than ever. Last year, "33 million went camping and another 32 million went for day hikes"[2] according to data from the Sporting Goods Manufacturing Association.

In the United States, many of the national parks offers seasonal employment as tour guides and in other hospitality-related positions. Parks in the West are especially popular for visitors and employees alike, but there are also positions at more out-of-way parks. The same goes for state parks, although some of them are managed remotely and may only have a full-time ranger or two on staff. However, local ecotourism companies and groups offer guided tours through the parks. Some of the tours can be interesting, such as air boating through the Everglades or snowmobiling through Yellowstone. There are entire niche segments of ecotourism. For example, there are dozens of companies in the Northeast and New England that offer fall foliage tours, by foot, car, and bicycle. Some ecotours in the United States meld cultural aspects as well. The well-rounded tour guides combine the human history of the land with its natural history. There are tours that specialize in this niche as well. This is popular in the Southwest, particularly in Native American lands.

For the ecotourism industry, it's difficult to get an accurate salary range, because "salaries for ecotourism managers, operators and guides can be difficult to predict, because of vast differences between employers and the tourism market itself."[3] And ecotourism can be seasonal, especially in areas that are dependent on tourist traffic. Most positions also include free room and board, especially if you are working in remote locations and in foreign countries. And there can be a great deal of personal satisfaction when dealing with local populations and getting a chance to see a culture that you normally wouldn't by just hanging out at a tourist resort.

An ancillary career is as a consultant to hotels and lodging facilities, to help them upgrade their green credentials and consult with major chains on sustainable business practices. Green hotel certifications are now popping up in the larger hotels, even in areas that are undeniably not ecotourism destinations. Working as a green hotel operator is another career track that is increasing in demand, as hotels see the same benefit that companies do, in terms of marketing and economic impact, by going green. A number of hotels already have green programs, and others actually run specialized ecotours right from the hotel instead of outsourcing to tour companies. Green hospitality professionals can also design green vacation packages that are specifically tailored to certain regions or interests (such as a scuba diving trip or a birding vacation).

People interested in ecotourism jobs should have some general qualities. Fluency in a foreign language is essential for many of the ecotourism opportunities. Another thing is that ecotourism company employees, especially field guides, need to be in good shape for often arduous conditions. A goal-oriented, take-charge mentality is needed for working with some of the ecotourism operators in more remote locations. Education is not really a cornerstone. And a surprising number of universities offer degree programs in ecotourism. Most concentrate on the business aspects of running an ecotourism business; others are more in tune with the sustainability and cultural aspect of the career.

Job Resources/Organizations

- Adventure Jobs (www.lookingforadventure.com). This Web site promises unique job opportunities—from ranch hands to charter boat mates to summer camp counselors. A good chunk of these positions are outdoorsy/ecotourism-related jobs.
- Back Door Jobs (www.backdoorjobs.com/). The Web site is billed as "short-term job adventures," and the openings deliver on that promise. This is a clearinghouse for jobs in environmental education, ecotourism, and hospitality. The two things the jobs have in common are that all are seasonal, part-time, or internships, and they all are outdoors jobs—no sitting behind a computer at a desk all day long here. The positions are mainly in the United States, but work-abroad programs are also featured.
- Bird Jobs (www.osnabirds.org/on/ornjobs.htm). Part ecotourism-related, part ecological science-related, the Orthinological

Association's Web site has a listserv for all jobs relating to birding, bird research, bird protection, and bird habitat conservation.

- Cyber-Sierra's Natural Resources Job Search (www.cyber -sierra.com/nrjobs/index.html). This site has a lot of outdoors green jobs, such as in forestry and ecotourism. The site also breaks down employment into summer jobs, nonprofits, internships, and so on. It's a good site for those looking to work in the great outdoors.
- EcoTour Jobs (www.ecotourjobs.com/). This is a fairly simple job site that not only lists available positions in the industry, but also with ecotourism companies in various regions worldwide.
- Ecotourism Job Centre (ecoclub.com/jobs). This Web site is part of the International Ecotourism Club. Listings are updated regularly and feature ecotourism jobs worldwide. Of particular import is a master search engine that has thousands of ecotourism undergraduate and postgraduate degree programs from universities all over the world.
- Ecotourism Jobs (www.ecotourismjobs.org). This free site lists a large number of foreign ecotourism jobs. The homepage warns of unscrupulous foreign ecotourism companies that are working for their own profit rather than the welfare of the natural communities to which they take their tours. So it's safe to say that many of these jobs are for environmentally responsible companies.
- Great Adventures (www.great-adventures.com/know/plan/work.html). This site has links to various ecotourism jobs, volunteer opportunities, internships, and outdoor/adventure jobs across the globe, including Antarctica. Some links are especially helpful, giving out information about working in countries on a temporary basis or in a long-term position.
- The International Ecotourism Society (www.ecotourism.org). The Society is dedicated to promoting sustainable, responsible travel to areas, supporting the local populace, and preserving the environment. The site has a veritable cornucopia of resources, links, articles, events, and marketing opportunities.
- Responsible Travel (www.responsibletravel.com/). This is a huge, U.K.-based site that advertises hand-selected responsible travel tours, family vacations, package deals, cruises, scuba adventures, and a variety of other responsible packages. These vacations "respect destinations and local people." This is a good site for job seekers looking to see what companies run these type

of tours and offer vacation packages. The travel company itself also advertises job openings and internships in the company.

Waste Management

What happens to your cans and bottles after they're dropped off at the nearest recycling facility? And, more important, what types of jobs are available in waste management, specifically recycling, now such an integral part of life for tens of millions of Americans. The recycling industry, like many others, goes through boom-and-bust cycles, but recycling is only getting more popular, and there needs to be services and companies to step in and fill that demand for service. Low-level sorters and factory workers are not in as demand as much as sorting machines, and more streamlined operations are taking over the labor-intensive part of prepping the recyclable materials.

Most jobs in the waste management industry are with municipal solid waste departments. Private waste management companies are another area for potential jobs. In some locations, such as New York City, private waste companies provide a lot of the services. There are jobs in positions ranging from administrative to environmental engineers and sustainability professionals. A lot of municipal recycling and waste management departments have public education and outreach programs. They also have a large number of permit requirements that environmental scientists and consultants help them keep up with. Solid waste facilities also need machinists and crane operators.

The job outlook is fair for lower-level employees, especially at municipal facilities. It's often hard to find job openings because of the security of the public sector. Private waste hauling outfits and recycling facilities are on the rise, and, with more and more communities mandating recycling but with shrinking budgets, more of the collections, disposal, and recycling will be done by contracted firms. Salaries can range from minimum wage for low-level sorters and workers, going up to an average of around $50,000 for recycling facility operators. Most recycling and waste management positions require little formal education, and some facilities offer on-the-job training and advanced certification programs.

- Recycling Jobs (www.recyclingjobs.com). The name says it all; this is the site for recycling opportunities. The jobs include engineers, environmental coordinators, site managers, education and outreach, and a variety of administrative positions.

- Resource Recycling (www.resource-recycling.com). This is a journal for recycling professionals; subscribers have access to job listings in the field.
- Waste and Recycling Jobs (www.environmental-expert.com/jobs). The site features national and international jobs in the waste industry, from recycling to hazardous waste disposal.

Green Interior Design

This is a subset of the green building category. Green interior design is the practice of using sustainable materials and environmentally friendly products and décor to decorate residences, businesses, schools, and hospitals. Green interior designers must be on top of the latest sustainable materials available and must be able to meet the traditional design needs of clients without sacrificing the green aspect of their job. It's a challenging career that combines creativity, business acumen (over one-quarter of interior designers are self-employed), scientific literacy (including computer skills), and a genuine flair for design. It's a job that you might not think would be a green career, but the job outlook is rosy.

Education is essential. Often a bachelor's degree from an art institute or design school is preferred. There are close to 250 educational institutions across the country that offer degree programs in interior design, and many of them are incorporating green design as a large part of the curriculum. There are a number of professional associations for interior designers, and, as with some of the other more advanced-level green jobs, associations are a great tool for networking and finding new opportunities. Another important part of education and training is licensing. Over 25 states require interior designers to have a special license. The need to get this license falls on the decorator, so you must do your homework in the state where you plan on working.

Job outlook for interior designers in general is positive. There is an expected increase of 20 percent from 2006 to 2016 in general interior design, although, according to the U.S. Bureau of Labor, "keen competition is expected for jobs because many talented individuals are attracted to this occupation."[4] Salaries are also competitive, but self-employed professionals can make either more or less depending on their business. As green building becomes more the norm than the exception, it's anticipated that green designers will be a bigger part of the interior design world.

General Resources

- Gleicher Design Group (gleicherdesign.com/). This is a green design firm in New York City. It's an example of the type of larger companies that are hiring green interior designers.
- Green Design Consulting (greendesignconsulting.com/). This consulting company works on coming up with green design schemes for residential interiors. It also works with the builders and remodelers to reduce materials that contain potential indoor air pollutants. It also delves into *feng shui* design schemes. Feng shui design, although it is not green per se, often works in tandem with the goals of green interior designers.
- Green Home Guide (www.greenhomeguide.com). The guide is simply a resource for consumers to look at which companies offer green products and where they can find green interior designers to help make their eco-living a little easier. It's also a great place for people interested in the field to find out who is doing design and which companies are working in the field for furniture, carpeting, paint, curtains, and so on. The green designer search engine is only for seven metro areas as of mid-2009.
- Interior Design Jobs (interiordesignjobs.sellisp.com/). This site is a clearinghouse for general interior design jobs, with plenty of green jobs in the mix.
- Maggie Wood (www.maggiewood.com). A perfect example of a company filling a green niche, Maggie Wood Design & Consulting helps homeowners make their house green, whether through interior design, or from the time the owners start to dream up the plans for their house. It's an example of a smaller interior design company.

Green Food Industry

Walk into any major supermarket these days and you'll undoubtedly see organic and natural foods in the frozen section and on the shelves. Supermarket chains from Wal-Mart to Publix are expanding their selections. Even smaller chains are adding a greater selection of organic food products to their shelves. The products are found in "73 percent of conventional supermarkets."[5] Major natural food chains, such as Whole Foods, have brought the idea of a natural food supermarket to the mainstream. Organic food products are expected to gain even greater market share over the next decade. Sales from organic products total over $1 billion per year. Within 20 minutes in driving distance from my house, there is a Whole Foods, two independent natural foods markets, a Publix Greenways store, and a dozen or so supermarkets with large organic/natural foods sections—not to mention farmers' markets and restaurants that specialize in green and locally produced foods.

Organic is a designation that has to meet certain criteria. The labels can be as confusing as the vast vernacular used to delineate the products. *Locally produced* is not the same as organic, which is not the same as *natural*. The mix is heady to be sure. Working in such a topsy-turvy world is not always easy. Farming never is. The jobs in this sector range from all farm-related employment to agricultural researchers, organic product buyers for food chains, food writers, chefs who use locally produced and organic ingredients in their cooking, and a number of other food-related professions that embrace the sustainable ethic.

This ethic goes from using less pesticides and herbicides to raising livestock humanely and feeding them natural feeds rather than subsidizing corn-based feeds. Sustainable seafood is a whole other category. Aquaculture, for its shortcomings and own environmental issues, is increasing in popularity as wild fish stocks are collapsing commercially. Even for the wild fish stocks that are in good shape, there are tough rules regulating the types of gear, size of the fish, seasons, and pounds allocated to the commercial sector. Jobs in the fisheries industry and aquaculture generally aren't near the top of the pay scale, and aren't green jobs, per se, but they overlap with some of the other job categories.

Organic food jobs can come in a variety of guises: proprietors of natural food stores, farmers' market organizers, organic farm workers, and sustainable fishermen. There are over 20,000 organic farms in the United States currently, not to mention thousands more examples of traditional farms that promote locally produced produce and sustainable practices. One surging job career is that of independent food manufacturers and specialty food item retailers. There are more organic and natural foods coming onto the market, and many are made by small companies. One popular way to enter this market is to refine traditional food products with organic ingredients. Another area that organic has been slow to get into is ethnic foods. There are options to bring entire ethnic cuisines into the organic food marketplace.

To this end, the rise of the celebrity chef and the glut of cooking shows on TV are giving organic, locally produced, and natural foods their biggest boost to date. Many of the chefs on shows such as *Top Chef* or on the Food

Network are using their pulpit, the TV test kitchen, to expound on the virtues of fresh, natural foods. They also talk at length about eating foods that are in season. The rationale behind this is that by eating foods in season, you reduce demand on foods trucked in from the other side of the country, or from foreign farmers, to meet the demand of apples in the dead of summer or summer squash in winter. This applies to chefs in restaurants who are beginning to eschew the traditional ways of cooking for new recipes and techniques that take the vast local resources and produce and bring that to the table. With these advocates, organic and natural food production is rising, and it offers the chance to be at the forefront. As an aside, being an organic or sustainable food chef is another viable green career; it is a career that does good things for the environment, and, by purchasing products from local farmers, you are stimulating the local economy far more than buying frozen fish from Taiwan.

Hard Sciences

For all the hype over new green jobs, job opportunities in the traditional sciences are growing as well. Scientific fields, from biology to oceanography to chemistry to biotechnology, are seeing demand rise. An older generation of scientists is retiring with fewer younger recruits coming up behind to fill positions, similar to what is going on the engineering industry. And there is the general growth of scientific research and development in the United States. For all the talk about the poor state of science in the United States, it is still the dominant country for science worldwide, although education issues need to be addressed, because the United States is losing ground to the European Union, China, and India.

A career in science is such a broad topic to cover. Research positions, positions in academia, government scientific regulatory agencies, private consulting companies, NGOs, military—these are all potential areas for employment. Science is crossing over into other fields as well, merging with behavioral analysis and economics to create new hybrids of jobs. The scientific fields are equally as vast, but certain areas are offering increasing promise for job growth.

Among those promising careers, genetics, biotechnology, and microbiology are growing as we understand more about the complex interactions of genes and look to genetic material as being the source of potential cures for a variety of terminal and long-term diseases such as cancer and diabetes. Genetic manipulation will lead to newer methods of genetic therapies. Scientists are able to detect genetic markers for certain diseases and give patients an idea of their chances of developing a disease. Full DNA profiles are still expensive and not readily available, but that will change. In a few years, you'll be able to discover your whole genetic makeup and your proclivity for certain diseases as you age. And when you get a disease, the therapies will include working with your genetic makeup to turn on and off certain gene sequences to prevent or cure the disease. This was squarely in the realm of science fiction, but major advances in the last decade have brought this to reality. Like stem-cell research, there are ethical implications and the fact that many people will simply choose not to find out if they are going to have cancer later in life. But the opportunities for genetic researchers, microbiologists, and others in those fields are growing rapidly. Most of the work is in private companies and academic institutions, as well as in a few federal agencies. There is little if any public sector work outside of these federal agencies, although some state environmental and health departments may have openings for scientists in these fields.

Salaries for lab technicians are usually around the $20,000–$30,000 per year range, rising as the techs become assistants and then researchers. Labs for private companies pay more than the federal government, but government jobs can be rewarding from a research perspective. Partnering with academic institutions, the research focus at public agencies is often wide, covering a swath of topics, whereas private companies are usually more narrow in their research, although funding at private companies can be higher. It all really depends on the specifics of the institution and the type of research being done.

- National Institutes of Health Jobs (www.jobs.nih.gov/vacancies/ sciencejobs.htm). The nation's primary medical research agency, the National Institute has job openings ranging from biologists, chemists, microbiologists, technicians, to administration.
- New Scientist Jobs (www.newscientistjobs.com/jobs/). The magazine's job site has free registration where you can upload your résumé, search through jobs in the United States and internationally by science field, and sign up for a news feed. The *New Scientist* is one of the premier science news publications.
- Science Careers (sciencecareers.sciencemag.org/). A service of the esteemed scientific journal *Science*, the site is a mixed bag of science positions in private companies and academia.
- Top Research Jobs (www.topresearchjobs.com/). This site lists a variety of public, private, and academic research positions. The

positions are mainly in the United States, but some international ones are mixed in as well.

Even More

Green activist: There has been a lot of references so far in this book to NGOs and environmental activist organizations. These can be perfect places to seek green employment because many of these groups are leading the charge for the government and corporations to become greener and taking the lead in addressing climate change and other environmental concerns. Working for these organizations can give the employee a real sense of worth and the feeling of doing something right, a sense of accomplishment, which is probably the driving force behind many of the people who seek employment in this underrated job sector. When green jobs are mentioned in the media or when in-depth articles are written giving the job outlook for green jobs, NGOs are rarely mentioned. These groups can range from the in-your-face, controversial antics of Greenpeace to smaller local nonprofits that work behind the scenes to preserve a small park or clean up a body of water.

In the environmental community, there are those that see the activists as essential for bringing environmental issues to the public's attention and others who see them as loudmouths who do little but stir a backlash against professionals in the field. This is really how these groups are viewed in the environmental science field, from a professional's point of view. But many NGOs work together with public agencies and private companies and look toward a combined effort to address environmental concerns. For the job seeker who is looking to start out in the green field, working for an NGO can be a rewarding experience.

Groups that work in restoration use volunteers and low-level employees as field help, giving them a taste of the field-work aspect of environmental science jobs. Some NGOs are more concerned with public education and nurture their talent to become better public presenters. These groups often speak up at public agency hearings and to lawmakers. It's vital for workers in an NGO to be familiar not only with general scientific issues but also with the specifics of certain cases or issues that are being addressed. Working for these groups, especially the ones that are involved with the local community, is also a great networking opportunity.

The job outlook for these groups is good, with one caveat. A lot of these groups are nonprofit and are financed by donations, grants, and direct funding from government agencies. In times of economic uncertainty, donations, grant funding, and government budgets all decrease, adding pressure on the nonprofits. Because of this funding, the pay, especially for lower-level employees, is usually lower than at comparable public agencies and private companies. But some of the larger NGOs do offer competitive pay, as well as full-benefit packages. It's essential, again, to research the organizations before you apply. Many of the environmental NGOs serve as jumping-off points for people who go into other job sectors, so there is a rate of turnover at some environmental organizations.

The following are some of the larger environmental NGOs and ones that regularly have job openings:

- Earthwatch (www.earthwatch.org). Earthwatch's mission is protection of environmental and cultural resources through research, education, and conservation. The group offers funding for scientists, outreach programs in remote outposts and in Third World countries, as well as training programs. The Web site lists job positions, both domestic and foreign, as well as internship opportunities.
- National Audubon Society (www.audubon.org). The Audubon Society is about more than birds. Although bird management and protection are the cornerstones of the organization, the organization has moved into general wildlife protection and conservation of essential habitat. Audubon relies heavily on volunteers, and it can be a great intern opportunity. The Society has chapters nationwide, and its Web site has a career section with job opening and internship information.
- National Wildlife Federation (NWF) (www.nwf.org). Based in Virginia, the NWF has offices across the country, and its Web site features job listing you can search by location. The NWF is committed to protecting the wildlife of the United States and has also recently taken up action related to global climate change.
- The Nature Conservancy (www.nature.org). The Nature Conservancy is one of the largest private landowners in the United States. Together with public and private partnerships, it manages millions of acres of critical and threatened habitats in the United States and worldwide. The Conservancy also works to protect undersea resources. The careers at the Conservancy are in science, research, conservation management, fundraising, outreach, and other fields. The Conservancy offers competitive benefits packages and continued professional training.

- Rainforest Action Network (www.ran.org). The Network's mission has evolved from protecting the rainforest to taking on many of the major challenges—climate change, oil use, water resources. Headquartered in San Francisco, the Network offers volunteer positions and internships as well as occasional full-time job openings.
- Sierra Club (www.sierraclub.org). The Sierra Club was founded in 1892, making it one of the oldest environmental organizations. It has chapters worldwide and is active in promoting alternative energy, climate change issues, environmental policy, preserving endangered lands, and protecting endangered species. The group's Web site has a careers page. Although the jobs are at an NGO, the Sierra Club offers a good benefits package and even a pension and 401(k) plan. Job openings range from administrative to technical, fundraising, outreach, and communication.
- Tampa BayWatch (www.tampabaywatch.org). I may be dropping in a plug here for an organization I have a lot of personal ties with, but it is a model of a small nonprofit whose works compete with NGOs five times as large. BayWatch works primarily with school groups and thousands of volunteers on restoration projects around Tampa Bay, from salt marsh plantings, to sea grass transplanting, to oyster bar creation.
- Union of Concerned Scientists (www.ucsusa.org). The Union works closely with lawmakers in bringing scientific concerns to public policy. The group's job openings are primarily in Washington DC. It also regularly recruits volunteers. It's a perfect place to become familiar with environmental law and policy.
- The Wilderness Society (wilderness.org). The Wilderness Society works primarily on preserving swaths of essential habitat through legislation. Recently, the Society has also added climate change to its core issues.
- Wildlife Conservation Society (www.wcs.org). The Society is headquartered at the world famous Bronx Zoo in New York City. It has a presence at other zoos across the country and works on programs in over 60 countries worldwide—protecting wildlife species, revitalizing populations, and protecting habitat. Careers are full-time, seasonal field jobs (often abroad), internships, and volunteer opportunities.

Green fashion designers: Organic cotton shirts are available in your local mall. Bamboo shirts are popular warm weather alternatives to synthetic fibers. Hemp clothing is no longer the domain of the patchouli oil crowd. Organic materials have made their way into beauty products, from shampoo to soap. Designers are hawking their wares at local farmers' markets, natural food stores, green expos, on the catwalk at fashion shows, and showing up in upscale boutiques, where they will no doubt become the next "it" item for the hipsters. But green fashion will likely not go away with next season's line but become a constant feature of clothes, beauty products, and accessories.

Environmentally sustainable fashion is a growing sector of the always interesting fashion industry. And the green designers who are leading the charge are taking their sustainability ideas to new heights. There are a number of blogs and Web sites that are tracking the changes. Because this is a very new field, it's difficult to give an accurate job outlook, but worldwide use of organic materials in clothing increased by over 15 percent from 2004 to 2008.[6] Salaries can range across the board, depending on cities where the designer is based or on sales for self-starters with their own business. Because there are only a few fashion schools that offer green design courses, education is still the usual channel for designers. This is definitely an area for adventurous and entrepreneurial designers looking to make names for themselves in a field that is in the January of its year.

- Eco Fabulous (www.ecofabulous.com). This is a green lifestyle blog that posts the best in interior design, clothing, green gifts, green design trends, and beauty products that are cruelty-free and use organic ingredients. The fashion is not only aimed at women—there's an eco-man section as well.
- EcoSalon (www.ecosalon.com). This whole-green site concentrates on all aspects of green living and design, featuring up-and-coming designers, the latest green products, style schemes for your house, and other green ideas. Sites such as this one are good ways for job seekers to look at who is doing what—which companies are making green design products, which fashion designers are working in green, and what areas of the country are the hot spots for green design careers.
- Evolved Fashion (www.evolvedfashion.com). Evolved Fashion is a blog for fashionistas and spa-a-holics looking for green fashions and beauty supplies. The site also tests out some of the products it blogs about and features interviews with green designers.
- Fabulously Green (fabgreen.com). Run by designer Stephanie Zhong, this site gives the fashion design job seeker a good

account of the new products, styles, materials, and workplace
changes in the green design field. The site also looks at everything from baby fashion to lighting schemes, interior design,
and green furniture.

Green furniture makers: A small subset of home furnishings, the green
sector is primarily dominated by smaller niche manufacturers and
designers. But that may soon change as more and more retailers, including store such as Target, Crate and Barrel, and furniture giant Ikea, are
recognizing the value of going green and are bowing to consumer
demand. Ikea has been especially active in the green push. In January
2009, plans were announced to build a 95,000-square-foot manufacturing
plant in the small town of Dandridge, Tennessee. The company building
the facility is BJS North America, a Swedish-headquartered company.
They plan on building a variety of green furnishings and will ship to
Ikea. The furniture retailer "has, to a great degree, influenced the domestic furniture makers' push toward green."[7]

Green furniture uses recycled or sustainable wood products, nontoxic
paints and stains, and sustainable fabrics. Some designers specialize in
taking old pieces of furniture and reusing them in new creations. Many
furniture designers are also based in the United States, adding the locally
produced motif. That's especially helpful because the U.S. furniture-
making industry has been hit by cheap imports from China, and companies in furniture hot spots such as North Carolina are disappearing. The
previously mentioned Dandridge plant is an example of the commitment
to use local labor in order to reduce shipping costs and greenhouse gas
emissions in shipping for companies dedicated to sustainability.

Green furniture design and manufacturing creates a nice synergy
with green interior design, green building, and green fashion. It's
another example of the tight interconnectedness of the green industry.
Green furniture can be sleek and ultra-modern, but another large segment is the craftsman look, one that resonates with bungalow dwellers
everywhere. Soon, even cheap college dorm furniture will be going
green.

General trade educations in furniture-making can readily be applied
to green furniture. Jobs include working on the assembly lines for larger
factories or carving out individual pieces for the smaller firms. Designers are also in demand, especially those with a holistic approach to green
design—from ergonomics to recyclable materials, to organic coverings.
Most of the jobs are on the lower-end of the pay scale for the larger factories, but some niche manufacturers with high-end luxury buyers can

make more because their pieces fetch a higher price at the retailer. An example of that is Robert Craymer, a well-known furniture designer from California who designed green furnishings for the Golden Globe Awards and who has appeared on HGTV and is a favorite of Oprah. His flagship store in Los Angeles is the first "one-stop furniture store that will design, manufacture and retail an organic and all natural 'Eco' line of furniture."[8]

Like most green versions of jobs that have been around for years (or centuries, in the case of furniture), green furniture design and manufacturing is a relatively new idea that is just starting to take shape. In the past year, more and more retailers have been offering green furnishings, and manufacturers are coming out with more mass market green items. Even though there is no official job outlook for this career track, it's safe to assume that the growing trend of everything green will buoy up the green furniture industry as well.

CHAPTER 11

A FINAL NOTE

Working in the environmental field today has its challenges, but it is far more rewarding than frustrating. Part of that is the fact that there is a real sense of promise and of excitement in the industry. For the first time, the environmental sector is near the top of person-job predictors for growth in the future. And there is support from government agencies and the White House. Some green jobs may not have any relationship with traditional environmental science positions, but they are all part of the same big tent, a tent large enough to accommodate plumbers and biochemists, hydrologists, and solar panel installers. And it's this push for science that is so exciting. A recent issue of *Seed* magazine sported this title on the cover: "Science can fix this." And it's true. All the environmental issues we are currently facing can be addressed, abated, and even conquered by utilizing the best and brightest, along with the driven and hard-working, to make a real difference. Sure, part of it reminds people of a simple pep talk at times, but it's true. Science and technological innovation are the driving forces behind the economy to a large extent and will be even bigger contributors in the future. And that future is closer than most people realize. When the economy starts its recovery, whatever form that will take, some career categories will be wiped out or decimated beyond repair. And in the aftermath, science will drive the new economic engine of a green economy.

It's apparent that green jobs are a wide and varied topic that extends across a variety of skill sets, knowledge bases, and educational experiences.

The promise of green jobs and the reality may not be exactly in sync, but that's to be expected with any new concept. Green job training programs are just starting to turn out students into a weak job market with the highest rate of unemployment in a generation. But that was part of the design. Getting these workers trained to do the jobs that will be the benchmark of the recovery means giving them a head start to get ahead of the curve.

It won't be an easy ride. There will be the naysayers who point at the job predictions and shake their finger at anything less than what was promised. They won't take into account the fact that most of these jobs are developing and need time to grow and take hold. Another issue that may derail some of the green revolution may simply be the lack of good education and training. For all the training programs and educational opportunities that were outlined in the previous chapters, American kids are still woefully behind many other countries when it comes to test scores in math and science.

Issues will need to be resolved as the programs grow and as the job market shakes out from the surge of interest in these positions, as well as changes in the job market after the recession is over. Energy prices may fluctuate again, bringing some dips and rises in the job outlook for alternative energy, although that is being mitigated on a daily basis by the surging number of government-sponsored programs and funding options for renewable energy. Things that will be set for the future are the jobs that really truly have sustainability and the green ethos as a core part of their description. These are the jobs that will be giving economic hope to disadvantaged populations and displaced workers. It's these jobs that will make the difference for rural communities that are reeling from the closing of a manufacturing plant or for a Detroit auto worker who is out of a job at the factory where he worked for two decades.

Current high school or college students who are looking to refine their education or go into green careers will find that the opportunities for study are increasing every semester. Environmental science is now a major in hundreds of schools, from community colleges to Ivy League universities. Green jobs training for the more technical positions and degrees in alternative energy are showing up in certain regions of the country where those jobs are most likely to appear. The training opportunities for people looking to switch careers are more accessible than ever, from in-person and on-site training to online certificate programs. There has never been an easier time to find the additional training needed to move into these new job sectors. And with more companies and institutions and governments offering training programs, the more affordable the programs are becoming. Even job training with a group such as the Oakland Green Job Corps, which is investing tens of thousands in each student, will see those costs drop and the benefit increase as the students come back and mentor the next class, giving the new students practical advice on working in a green job sector.

Although this book gave a comprehensive overview of the green job sector and the opportunities available for people interested in an environmental career, it did not discuss the most important green job category—because it hasn't been invented yet. The thing to keep in mind when reading through the various environmental career tracks is that many of these jobs are developing as we speak. This is the time to get in on the ground floor, to take one of these job tracks and run with it. For many of these, especially in the technical and professional positions, the ability to move from career to career is within reach because of the interconnecting skill sets that connect so many green jobs. A biologist can get into ecotourism, then into water quality, then go to school for an engineering degree, and then get into green building, on and on. Green careers may not end up being the panacea that some are predicting, but they are certainly here to stay. This is not a fad that will be gone in a few years. Most of these career paths will continue whether individual job descriptions change or as technology changes; having the knowledge and basic skill sets will make it easier to adapt.

And that brings up one other good point. The days of working 25 years in a factory doing the same thing are about gone. Adaptability and flexibility are the new order of the day, and the green career sector is no different. That flexibility extends to the green careers themselves. The next big thing may be a new technology that comes out of one of the many existing companies in the field, or it could be from the job that you create, in the company that you found, or from working on the product that you develop. The green sector has the flexibility to accommodate a wide cross-section of positions and the flexibility to address environmental issues as they arise.

NOTES

Introduction

1. http://en.wikipedia.org/wiki/Brundtland_Commission.
2. http://www.times.org/archives/2005/pollock.pdf.
3. http://www.youtube.com/watch?v=uQ058zrZyTo.

Chapter 1

1. Schere, Ron (2009, June 10). "Report: 'Green Jobs' Outpacing Traditional Ones." *Christian Science Monitor.*
2. Friedman, T. L. (2008). *Hot, Flat, and Crowded.* Farrar, Straus & Giroux, New York, p. 235.
3. Kolbert, E. (2009, June 29). "The Catastrophist." *The New Yorker.*
4. Roberts, G. (2002, March 30). "Islanders Face Rising Seas with Nowhere to Go." *Sydney Morning Herald.* Retrieved on February 3, 2009 from http://www.smh.com.au/articles/2002/03/29/1017206152551.html.
5. Retrieved on June 11, 2009 from http://www.pewtrusts.org/news_room_detail.aspx?id=53254.
6. Retrieved on July 5, 2009 from http://www.mnn.com/business/green-jobs/blogs/secretary-solis-on-green-jobs.
7. Llewellyn, Bronwyn. (2009, June 15,). "Green Jobs Q&A: What Is the Government Doing to Help?" Retrieved on June 29, 2009 from http://www.mnn.com/business/green-jobs/stories/green-jobs-q-a-what-is-the-government-doing-to-help.

8. Ibid.

9. Ian Thompson interview, April 2009.

10. Duggan, Will. E-mail to author, Feb. 3, 2009.

Chapter 2

1. Walsh, Bryan. "What Is a Green Collar Job, Exactly?" *Time*. May 26, 2008. Retrieved on March 20, 2009 from http://www.time.com/time/ health/article/0,8599,1809506,00 .html.

2. Greenhouse, Steven. (2008). "Millions of Jobs of a Different Collar." Retrieved on April 17, 2009 from http://www.nytimes.com/2008/03/ 26/business/businessspecial2/26collar.html?ref=businessspecial2.

3. Makower, Joel, "Will Green Jobs Become the New Greenwash?" Retrieved on April 14, 2009 from http://makower.typepad.com/ joel_makower/2009/02/will-green-jobs-become-the-new-greenwash.html.

4. Center on Wisconsin Strategy. (2009). *Greener Pathways*.

5. Gehrman, Elizabeth. (2007, November 18). "Hot Jobs in a Green Economy." *The Boston Globe*.

6. Retrieved on June 1, 2009 from http://www.bp.com/productlanding .do?categoryId=7041&contentId=7046652.

7. Retrieved on May 1, 2009 from http://libertyhill.typepad.com/ main/2009/04/los-angeles-adopts-landmark-green-jobs-ordinance- .html.

8. http://apolloalliance.org/about/mission/.

9. Goldenberg, Suzanne. (2009, June 10). "Green Collar Job Creation 'Outstripped Traditional Sectors in US.'" *The Guardian*.

10. Hargreaves, Steve. (2009). "Renewables: America's Next Heavy Industry." CNNMoney.com. Retrieved May 30, 2009 from http://money.cnn .com/2009/05/21/news/economy/midwest_renewables/index.htm? section=money_topstories.

11. Retrieved on June 26, 2009 from http://www.michigan.gov/ nwlb/0,1607,7-242-48049---,00.html#1.

12. Retrieved on June 3, 2009 from: http://www.txenergyfuture.org/.

13. "Yellow Light on Green Jobs." *A Report by the U.S. Subcommittee on Green Jobs and the New Economy*. 2009.

14. Shore, Sandy. (2009, June 26), "Where Are the Renewable Jobs?" The Associated Press.

15. Merlino, John. E-mail to author, Feb. 5, 2009.

16. Morris, A. P., W. T. Bogart, A. Dorchak, and R. E. Meiners. (2009). "Green Jobs Myths." *University of Illinois Law & Economics Research Paper No. LE09-001*.

17. Retrieved on June 20, 2009 from http://sierraclub.typepad.com/compass/2008/10/q-a-with-van-jones.html.

18. Retrieved on June 24, 2009 from http://www.reuters.com/article/gwmEnergy/idUS166852870120090625.

Chapter 3

1. Shore, Sandy. (2009, June 26).

2. Retrieved on June 1, 2009 from http://www.greenenergyjobs.com/career-guide/water-jobs/index.php.

3. Araj, Elie, E-mail to author, May 2, 2009.

4. Krzys, Bernard. (2009). "From the Publisher's Desk." *Water Utility Infrastructure Management.*

5. Knight, W. (2008). *Engineering Has Ceased to Be* . . . Retrieved on September 15, 2008 from http://kn.theiet.org/magazine/issues/0816/skills-0816.cfm.

6. Cassidy, S. (2008). *CBI Sounds Alarm at Lack of Engineering Students.* Retrieved on September 15, 2008 from http://www.independent.co.uk/news/education/education-news/cbi-sounds-alarm-at-lack-of-engineering-graduates-829926.html.

Chapter 4

1. The addition of nuclear is a controversial topic. A lot of former activists who stood up in arms over nuclear power now see its use as an alternative energy to oil and coal. For the purposes of this book, nuclear will not be discussed, but there are excellent resources available for people interested in this energy. I'd recommend starting with the Nuclear Energy Institute and the Nuclear Power Institute. The federal government also has resources on nuclear power.

2. Howell, K. (2009, April 13). "Natural Gas: Dramatic Growth Seen in Unconventional Plays." Retrieved on July 3, 2009 from http://www.eenews.net/public/Greenwire/2009/04/13/6.

3. Retrieved on June 29, 2009 from http://www.calgaryherald.com/Technology/Shocking+energy+bill/1742947/story.html.

4. Ian Thompson interview, April 2009.

5. Chapo, Richard. "Disadvantages of Alternative Energy." Retrieved on April 24 from http://ezinearticles.com/?Disadvantages-of-Alternative-Energy&id=523873.

6. Hayward, Tony. (2009). "In Tough Times, Investing in Both the Energy and Environment." *World Energy Magazine.*

7. Millington, Pat, E-mail to author, April 10, 2009.

8. Shore, Sandy. 2009.

9. http://www.cted.wa.gov/site/974/default.aspx.

10. Kreiss, Fritz. E-mail to author, March 11, 2009.

11. Merlino, John. E-mail to author, Feb. 5, 2009.

12. Sutter, John D. (2009, March 2). "Growing Excitement, Expectations for Green Jobs Corps." CNN.com. Retrieved on May 3, 2009 from http://www.cnn.com/2009/LIVING/03/02/green.jobs.training/index.html?iref=mpstoryview.

13. Thurston, 2009.

14. Retrieved on June 1, 2009 from http://www.msnbc.msn.com/id/27339064/.

15. Machetta, J. (2009, May 27). "Obama's Green Jobs Adviser: Missouri a Common-Sense Location for Expansion." Retrieved on June 23, 2009 from http://www.missourinet.com/gestalt/go.cfm?objectid=82E570A1-5056-B82A-3743EBF489130870.

16. Retrieved on April 23, 2009 from http://www.evo.com/content/2827/solar_basics_-_how_much_does_a_home_solar_system_cost.

17. Retrieved on May 28, 2009 from http://www.boston.com/bostonworks/galleries/green_jobs1118?pg=13.

18. Fitzgerald, Beth. (2009). "N.J. Poised to Grow Green Jobs." Retrieved on March 12, 2009 from http://www.njbiz.com/industry_article.asp?cID=7&aID=94742146.34507302.1008059.113855.6058038.907&aID2=77534.

19. EERE Network News. (2009, April 16). "More Jobs in the Wind Power Industry". *Mother Earth News*. Retrieved on June 14, 2009 from http://www.motherearthnews.com/ Renewable-Energy/More-Wind-Green-Jobs.aspx.

20. Retrieved on June 13, 2009 from http://www.kestrelwind.co.za/news_article.asp?ID=285.

21. Sassoon, David. March 11, 2008. "Ethanol: By the Way, You'll Need Water." Retrieved on February 15 from http://solveclimate.com/blog/20080311/ethanol-way-youll-need-water.

22. Bigelow, Bruce. January 9, 2009. "San Diego Biofuels Industry Gains Steam with R&D Consortium." Xconomy San Diego.

23. Pulsinelli, Olivia. "Higher Education Adapts for Tomorrow's Jobs." Retrieved on June 24, 2009 from http://www.mlive.com/business/west-michigan/index.ssf/2009/06/adapting_for_tomorrows_jobs.html.

24. Smith, Emily. (2009, May 4). "University May Offer Degree in Sustainable Practices." *Oregon Daily Emerald*.

Chapter 5

1. "Sears Tower Unveils Plans for a $350 Mil Facelift and a 'Net-Zero' Hotel." Retrieved on June 26, 2009 from http://www.reuters.com/ article/gwmBuildings/idUS425208861220090626.

2. Retrieved on June 1, 2009 from http://www.usgbc.org/.

3. Buhayer, N. (2009, July 1). Green Buildings Get Boost in Cap-and-Trade Bill. Message posted to http://blogs.wsj.com/environmentalcapital.

4. Araj. (2009, May 2).

5. Tuyn, William W. E-mail to author, February 25, 2009.

6. http://www.smartcommunities.ncat.org/greendev/gdintro.shtml.

7. Araj. (2009, May 2).

8. City of Chicago. "Green Alleys." Retrieved on June 1, 2009 from egov.cityofchicago.org.

9. Tuyn. (2009, February 25).

10. Avera, M. W. (2007, July 10). "Finding the Right Shade of Green." Retrieved on June 28, 2009 from http://www.topbuildingjobs.com/ news.php?articleID=26.

11. Krieger, Sari. (2008, November 16). "Green Gap." Retrieved on July 29, 2009 from http://online.wsj.com/article/SB122661046508725685 .html.

12. Millington. (2009, April 10).

13. Ibid.

14. Ibid.

15. Retrieved on June 30, 2009 from http://www.greenplanphiladelphia .com/.

Chapter 6

1. Environmental Leader. "SAB Miller Targets 24 Percent Reduction in Water Used in Brewing." Retrieved on July 5, 2009 from http:// www.environmentalleader.com/2009/07/03/sab-miller-targets-25 -reduction-in-water-used-in-brewing/.

2. Copeland, M. (2008, April 17). "Great Green Careers." *Fortune.*

3. Naggapan, P. (2008, July 20). *The New Green Focus For Future MBA's.* Retrieved from http://www.greenbiz.com/feature/2008/07/21/ new-green-focus-future-mbas.

4. Shah, A. (2009, February 13). "Green Mutual Funds Ride Wave of Popularity." *Smart Money.* Retrieved on June 3, 2009 from http://www .smartmoney.com/investing/mutual-funds/green-mutual-funds-ride -wave-of-popularity-22554/.

Chapter 7

1. Retrieved from http://dictionary.babylon.com/Green_Marketing, on June 16, 2009.

2. BNET editorial, "Understanding Green Marketing." Retrieved on June 2, 2009 from http://www.bnet.com/2410-13237_23-168370.html.

3. Afuwale, P. "Make Your Marketing Green!" Retrieved May 2, 2009 from http://www.marketingcrossing.com/article/220560/Make-Your-Marketing-Green-/.

4. Merlino. (2009, February 5).

5. Barnes, Ryan. "Can Business Evolve in a Green World?" Retrieved on May 23, 2009 from http://www.investopedia.com/articles/07/green -effect-business.asp?partner=forbes-hpm&viewed=1.

6. Retrieved June 20, 2009 from http://www.businesspundit.com/25 -big-companies-that-are-going-green/.

7. Ibid.

Chapter 8

1. Gehrman. (2007, November 18).

2. Copeland. (2008, April 17).

Chapter 9

1. Retrieved on June 17, 2009 from http://www.panda.org/?167022/ Going-green-is-where-the-jobs-are-new-study.

2. Swartz, S. (2009, June 29). "Are Developing Economies Getting Serious about Energy Efficiency?" *Wall Street Journal* blog. Retrieved on June 30, 2009 from http://blogs.wsj.com/environmentalcapital/2009/06/ 29/are-developing-economies-getting-serious-about-energy-efficiency/.

3. Kloosterman, K. (2009, April 28). "Try Renewable Energy Jobs for 'Green' Jobs in the Middle East." Retrieved from http://greenprophet .com/2009/04/28/8608/renewable-energy-jobs/.

4. Retrieved on July 1, 2009 from http://www.ret.gov.au/energy/ energy%20programs/RenewableEnergyFund/Pages/Renewable EnergyFund.aspx.

5. Eybers, J. (2008, August 15). "Development-Africa: Retailer Creates Jobs with Green Practices." Inter Press Service Agency.

6. Osavo, M. (2008, June 3). "Brazil: Climate Change Will Weaken Renewable Energy Sources." Retrieved on April 23, 2009 from http://ipsnews.net/news.asp?idnews=42642.

7. United Nations Environmental Programme. (2009, January 9). *Japan and the Republic of Korea Launch Green New Deals*. Press Release.

Chapter 10

1. Shafer, Jack. (2007, July 6). "Green Is the New Yellow." *Slate*.

2. Tomalin, T. (2009, June 2). "We're Here to Provide That Push out the Door." *St. Petersburg Times*.

3. Retrieved on June 29, 2009 from http://www.emagazine .com/view/?3945.

4. Retrieved on May 29, 2009 from http://www.bls.gov/oco/ ocos293.htm.

5. Retrieved on June 30, 2009 from http://www.boston.com/ boston-works/galleries/green_jobs1118?pg=10.

6. Ibid.

7. Brass, L. (2009, January 19). "Ikea Sources 'Green' Furniture for Dandridge." *Knoxville Business Journal*. Retrieved on June 1, 2009 from http://www.knoxnews.com/news/2009/jan/19/ikea-sources-green -furniture-dandridge/.

8. Retrieved on July 3, 2009 from http://www.robertcraymer .com/about.php.

Further References

Cleary, J., and A. Kopicki. (2009). Preparing the Workforce for a "Green Jobs" Economy. Prepared for: John J. Heldrich Center for Workforce Development.

Dolan, K. A. (2008, November 24). "Mr. Ethanol Fights Back." *Forbes,* 52–57.

Editors. (2008, November 24). Bright Ideas. *Forbes,* 126–130.

Environmental Protection Agency. (2009). *Green Jobs Training.* Washington, D.C.

Friedman, T. (2008). *Hot, Flat, and Crowded.* Farrar, Straus & Giroux, New York.

Greenpeace. (2009, July). *Guide to Greener Electronics.* Greenpeace: Washington, D.C.

Hometown Advantage. "Big Box Economic Studies." Retrieved June 24, 2009 from http://www.newrules.org/sites/newrules.org/files/images/bigboxstudies.pdf.

Jones, C. (2009, June 23). "Oakland Green Jobs Corps Grads Go to Work." *San Francisco Chronicle.*

National Public Radio. (2008, January 31). "Job Campaign Seeks a More 'Green' Work Force." *Tell Me More.* Podcast retrieved from http://www.npr.org/templates/story/story.php?storyId=18570232.

Pew Charitable Trusts. (2009). *The Clean Energy Economy.* Washington, D.C.

Phelan, B. (2009, February). "Ecology of Finance." *Seed,* 16–18.

Pollin, R., and J. Wicks-Lim. (2008). *Job Opportunities for the Green Economy: A State-by-State Picture of Occupations That Gain from Green Investments*. Political Economy Research Institute, University of Massachusetts, Amherst.

Stone, D. (2009, July 2). "America's Green Warriors." *Newsweek*.

Watson, R. (2008). *Green Building Impact Report 2008*. Prepared for Greenerbuildings.com.

Worldwatch Institute. (2008). *Green Jobs: Towards Decent Work in a Sustainable, Low-Carbon World*. Prepared for the United Nations Environmental Programme: Nairobi, Kenya.

Zappala, J. L. (2009, May 5). "10 Hot Green Job Industries to Watch in 2009." Retrieved on June 1, 2009 from http://www.msnbc.msn.com/id/30508202/?pg=1#Biz_GreenJobs.

INDEX

ABOUT THE AUTHOR

Scott M. Deitche is an environmental scientist and department manager for the Tampa office of Greenman-Pedersen, Inc. (GPI), an engineering firm. He has 15 years of experience in environmental management, stormwater management, water resources, and marine fisheries. Scott has presented at numerous environmental conferences and is active in professional environmental groups. A professional author, he has also appeared on A&E; The Discovery Channel; The History Channel; local NBC, CBS, ABC, and Fox affiliates; and local and national radio programs. Learn more at www.scottdeitche.com.